Sasha Fenton's Planets in Astrology
Discover the Power of the Planets!

Sasha Fenton's Planets in Astrology

Discover the Power of the Planets!

Sasha Fenton

ZAMBEZI PUBLISHING LTD
www.zampub.com

First published as "The Planets" in April 1994 in the UK
by The Aquarian Press
This revised paperback edition
published worldwide August 2014, by Zambezi Publishing Ltd
Plymouth, Devon (UK)
Tel: +44 (0)1752 367 300   Fax: +44 (0)1752 350 453
email: zambezipub@gmail.com   www.zampub.com

Text copyright © 1994 - 2014 Sasha Fenton
Sasha Fenton has asserted the moral right to be
identified as the author of this work.

British Library Cataloguing in Publication Data:
A catalogue record for this book is available from the British Library

ISBN: 978-1-903065-76-1

Illustrations copyright © 2014 Jan Budkowski,
and planet images courtesy of NASA/JPL
Typesetting by Zambezi Publishing Ltd, Plymouth

All rights reserved. No part of this publication may be reproduced, stored in a retrieval system, or transmitted in any form or by any means, electronic, mechanical, photocopying, recording or otherwise, whether currently existing or yet to be developed, without the prior written permission of the publishers. This book is sold subject to the condition that it shall not, by way of trade or otherwise, be lent, resold, hired out or otherwise circulated without the publisher's prior written consent, in any form of binding, cover or format other than that in which it is originally published, and without a similar condition being imposed on the subsequent purchaser.

Disclaimer: - This book is intended to provide general information regarding the subject matter, and to entertain. The contents are not exhaustive and no warranty is given as to accuracy of content. The book is sold on the understanding that neither the publisher nor the author are thereby engaged in rendering professional services, in respect of the subject matter or any other field. If expert guidance is required, the services of a competent professional should be sought.

Readers are urged to access a range of other material on the book's subject matter, and to tailor the information to their individual needs. Neither the author nor the publisher shall have any responsibility to any person or entity regarding any loss or damage caused or alleged to be caused, directly or indirectly, by the use or misuse of information contained in this book. If you do not wish to be bound by the above, you may return this book in original condition to the publisher, with its receipt, for a refund of the purchase price.

About the Author

Sasha Fenton became a professional astrologer, palmist and Tarot card reader in 1974, but wound down her consultancy when her writing took off. She has written 129 non-fiction books, and a ten years' worth of chapters for the Llewellyn Sun Sign books. Her sales now approach seven million copies, with translations into fifteen languages. In 2013, Sasha took to writing fiction and she is now producing a series of "Tudorland" novels, of which "Sophie's Inheritance" and "Lucy's Dilemma" are the first.

Having written stars columns for many papers and magazines over the years, including *Woman's Own* and the *Sunday People*, Sasha has also had her own radio and television programmes and has broadcast for many UK radio and television stations, as well as several in the USA, Australia and South Africa. She has taught, lectured and broadcast all over the world, including at the prestigious Mind, Body and Spirit Festivals in London, Sydney and Melbourne and in Johannesburg and Cape Town.

Sasha has been President of the "British Astrological and Psychic Society" (BAPS), Chair for the "Advisory Panel on Astrological Education", and a member of the Executive Council of the "Writers' Guild of Great Britain".

Sasha and Jan run Zambezi Publishing Limited and Stellium Ltd, producing books and ebooks of many different kinds. She is married to Jan Budkowski, and has two children and four grandchildren.

Contents

Introduction to the Planets	3
Chapter One: Astronomical Data	7
Chapter Two: Astrological Data	12
Chapter Three: The Personal Planets	17
Chapter Four: The Transpersonal Planets	31
Chapter Five: The Impersonal Planets	37
Chapter Six: Other Features on a Chart	48
Chapter Seven: The Sun through the Signs	52
Chapter Eight: The Moon through the Signs	64
Chapter Nine: The Personal Planets	74
Chapter Ten: The Transpersonal Planets	86
Chapter Eleven: The Impersonal Planets	94
Chapter Twelve: Dwarf Planets through the Signs	100
Chapter Thirteen: Angles, Hemispheres, Elements and Qualities	106
Chapter Fourteen: The Houses	113
Chapter Fifteen: Planets in Houses	120
Chapter Sixteen: Aspects	162
Chapter Seventeen: The Body and Astrology	165
Conclusion	166
Index	167

Introduction to the Planets

I wrote the original version of this book in 1993, and while that feels as though it were only yesterday, it's amazing to think that twenty years have actually passed since then. In the intervening years, manned and unmanned space travel have added much to our knowledge of the solar system, but how can we incorporate these new discoveries into our existing astrological framework? Astrologers look at everything, and sometimes perhaps at too many things, but eventually the situation shakes down to what actually works, and that's what I have focused on in this book.

I only cover natal charting in this book, but when you are ready to move on to predictive techniques, you'll find a 'Sasha' book for that as well. Is this shameless self-promotion? Maybe so – but my motive is what it's always been, which is to help those who want to understand this fascinating subject.

Let us spend a moment considering that old chestnut of, what does or doesn't make astrology work… Scientists and wannabe scientists are quick to point out that a small rock at the end of the solar system can't possibly exert any magnetic or electrical effect on mankind and they're probably quite right. The only explanation I've heard that makes any sense at all comes from my late friend, the wonderful Jon Dee. He used to say that everything in the universe, including us, seems to resonate to some kind of celestial timing device, but whether this is by accident or whether it's something that God created and arranged, is beyond any of us. For my part, after working with the planets for over four decades, I accept that the system works, and that's enough for me.

Basic Information

I use the terms "he" and "him" most of the time as it makes the text easier to read.

I give capitals to "named" objects, such as Mercury, Venus etc. but also to items that are an essential part of this book, such as the Sun, the Moon and the Earth.

The word "horoscope" means, "map of the hour", and a natal chart is like a snapshot of the sky at the moment that something comes into existence.

The time of a person's birth is taken from the "first cry", which is the moment the baby draws its first breath and starts to cry. It makes no difference if the birth is premature, late, induced or caesarean; it's the first cry that sets the chart in place.

Most people don't have an accurate time of birth, even when it is recorded somewhere, so you usually need to jiggle a chart around a bit (rectify it) to find the exact position for the ascendant.

Tools of the Trade

When I wrote my first book, it was already getting hard to suggest what a new astrologer should buy in the way of astrological equipment, but now it's impossible! The items below are the best I can suggest under the circumstances.

You will need two ephemeredes (I can't bring myself to say ephemerises...) - one for the 20th century and another for the first half of the 21st century. If your eyesight isn't great, I suggest that you buy *"The Astrolabe World Ephemeris 2001-2050 at Midnight"* because the typeface is clear. That particular ephemeris gives the position of Chiron and the asteroids on a daily basis as well as all the usual planetary data.

Whatever ephemeris you buy, ensure that it's for midnight rather than noon, because that will show you the picture for the whole twenty-four hours that you wish to examine. If you ever take the trouble to learn how to calculate a chart by hand, you will definitely want a midnight ephemeris, because a noon one adds layers of difficulty to the process.

I use the annual *"Raphael's Ephemeris"* for day-to-day work, because it's invaluable for checking planetary and lunar positions, ingresses, eclipses and so much more. It saves me from having to consult a massive tome when I only want a quick glance at something. Study it well, because it really does offer an amazing amount of information in addition to the usual daily planetary data

Software varies from very basic to extremely complex, and with the recent advent of tablets, more programs come onto the market all the time. I suggest you roam the Net or find apps and buy whatever takes your fancy. You'll probably end up buying one or two different products until you find one that suits you. You can set up and run off a few free charts from *Astro.com* (this is a very useful website all round), and there may be other sites that will allow you to do this. A great site for celebrity charts is *www.astrotheme.com*. It's a French site, but it's written in English and it's free to use. It contains the data for hundreds of British and American celebrities, in addition to the European ones, and it frequently updates itself with new faces. This site also contains a number of articles that are worth reading.

The most popular professional quality astrology software in the UK is Solar Fire, but some astrologers use Astrocalc, Winstar or Kepler. There must be hundreds of programs available in the USA, so the best thing I can suggest is to ask other astrologers what they recommend. I've bought and used most programs that have been available in the UK over the years, but I always come back to my favourite, which is Solar Fire, and I update it from time to time.

Depending upon what kind of astrology takes your fancy, you might want to check out celebrity charts or you might take an interest in historical events or people of the past. The birth of countries, cities and nations might fascinate you, as might politics or finance. You might be into the astrology of climate, or it may be sporting events or rock music that catches your fancy. You may wish to delve into the deeper aspects of psychology, or you may want to choose the right day to start something that's important to you. Each one of us uses our astrology to suit our own needs, and those needs can be different from one day to the next.

Chapter One: Astronomical Data

The Plane of the Ecliptic

Before telescopes were invented and astronomers understood the solar system, it was thought that the Sun travels round the Earth, making one complete circuit each year. The trajectory of this apparent circuit is called the "plane of the ecliptic", or more commonly the "ecliptic", and everything in astrology happens along this line.

The Zodiac

The ecliptic is divided into twelve equal segments of 30 deg. each. About two and a half thousand years ago, astrologers fitted these segments to those constellations that sat along the ecliptic. The constellation of Aries then fit the part of the zodiac that marked the spring equinox, but in the intervening years, the tilt and wobble of the Earth has made the constellations slip back by about 25 degrees. This phenomenon is called "the precession of the equinoxes". Nevertheless, stick to the standard zodiac signs, simply because the system works.

Western astrologers still use the ancient "tropical zodiac" because it works well for us, so for us, Aries still starts on the 20th of March at the time of the spring equinox. Hindu astrologers use "sidereal" astrology, which takes account of precession, but their astrology isn't quite the same as ours.

The Planets

For the sake of convenience, we call most of the celestial objects that we deal with "planets", regardless of whether we're talking about the Sun, the Moon, a planet or a dwarf planet.

The Solar System

The Solar system in astrology looks like this:

> The Sun
> The Moon
> Mercury
> Venus
> Mars
> Jupiter
> Saturn
> Uranus
> Neptune
> Pluto
> Chiron

Apart from the Moon, the above list shows the planets in order of distance from the Sun. Earth is excluded, and isn't part of basic astrological chart calculations.

Also Consider…

> The Earth
> Vesta
> Ceres
> The Nodes of the Moon

Several other planets have now been discovered far out in the Solar system, but they take so long to orbit the Sun that they aren't much use in readings. For instance, Eris is a dwarf planet that is larger than Pluto, but it's so far out that it takes about 500 years to orbit the Sun. I guess Eris might be useful to those who like history. The following story is typical of the kind of coincidence that so often occurs to those who are into astrology or spiritual matters. At the time of writing this book, Eris is at 21 deg. Aries. As it happens, I've just spent the last few months working on two novels that are partly set in modern times and partly in Tudor times. The Tudor era started when the Wars of the Roses came to an end and Henry the Seventh became the first Tudor king. Interestingly, Eris was at 21 deg. Aries then, too!

The Sun

The Sun's mean distance is 149.6 million kilometres from the Earth. It takes 26.9 Earth days to rotate on its axis, and its mean surface temperature is 5,700 degrees Celsius, rising to about 15 million degrees Celsius at the core. It emits electromagnetic radiation of various wavelengths, some of which are harmful, but the radiation of heat and light from the Sun makes life possible.

The Moon

The Moon's mean distance from the Earth, surface to surface, is 384,400 kilometres. It takes 27.32 days for the Moon to travel round the Earth, and also 27.32 days for it to rotate on its axis; therefore it always has the same face pointing towards the Earth. Its diameter is 3,475.6km and its temperature varies between plus 120 degrees and minus 153 degrees Celsius. The interior of the Moon is still hot enough to be made of molten rock, and there are about

3,000 moonquakes per year. The surface of the Moon is fatter on the side that faces the Earth, and it is also warmer on the Earth side. Water, methane, ammonia, hydrogen, sodium, silver and Mercury have now been discovered on the surface of the Moon.

The Moon and the Earth were both formed when the Solar system came into being. The Moon became attracted to the Earth's gravitational field and formed a double or binary planet system. The Moon is about a quarter the size of the Earth, and its surface area is about the size of Asia. Nevertheless, its mountains reach up to 8,000 metres, which is around the height of Mount Everest. There is no atmosphere on the Moon. The Moon is moving slowly away from the Earth.

The Planets

Mercury, Venus, Earth and Mars are "terrestrial" planets with solid centres. Mercury is the closest to the Sun, albeit still about 35 million miles (58 million kilometres) from the Sun, so its surface temperature on the side that faces the Sun is very high. Its surface is similar to that of the Moon. Being small, it has little gravity and therefore, little atmosphere. What does exist is mainly hydrogen and helium. Dense clouds of carbon dioxide and sulphuric acid cover Venus. The surface of the Earth is mainly covered by water and partially covered by cloud. Surprisingly, the Earth sometimes has up to five Moons, but only one large one. The others are called *Minimoons*, and tend to be captured asteroids whose complicated orbits keep them here for a while – up to a year or so – and then they wander away to be asteroids again. Earth's atmosphere comprises oxygen, carbon dioxide, nitrogen and water vapour. Mars is mainly rocky desert with polar ice caps that were once liquid. A very thin atmosphere consists of carbon dioxide, oxygen and water vapour. Mars has two Moons - Phobos and Deimos.

Jupiter is a huge ball of gas, containing liquid hydrogen and helium with some methane and ethane. Uranus and Neptune are composed of dust, swirling rocks and gas. Saturn, Uranus and Neptune all have ring systems, with many Moons and rocks orbiting around them. Uranus spins in the opposite direction to all the other planets, and its poles are on the east and west alignment, rather than north and south. Uranus alternates between presenting its poles and its equator to the Sun, so that each has a summer of forty-two years, followed by a forty-two-year winter.

Pluto has a very elongated orbit, which, at times, reaches far inside the orbit of Neptune. It is too small to have any atmosphere, although frozen methane has been discovered on its surface. Pluto has one very large Moon called Charon (pronounced like Sharon) that is about one-third its size, plus several tiny ones. Pluto and Charon form a binary planetary system, because they swing around a point that is somewhere between them. Pluto may be small and distant, but its astrological effect is massive.

Chiron is a dwarf planet that moves in an eccentric orbit between Uranus and Neptune.

Chapter Two: Astrological Data

Personal, Transpersonal and Impersonal Planets

In astrology, we consider the Sun, Moon, Mercury, Venus and Mars as *personal* planets. These are the closest planets to the Earth and they are concerned with personality and behaviour. Beyond the asteroid belt, you can find Jupiter and Saturn, which are called *transpersonal* planets.

These show how the subject copes with the opposing forces of expansion and limitation, and they are somewhat more concerned with external influences than personal behaviour. The outer planets of Uranus, Neptune and Pluto are called *impersonal* planets, as they have a generational influence rather than a strictly personal one on a natal chart, but no planet is ever really impersonal, because everything in a birthchart makes itself felt.

Retrograde Planets

It's easy to become familiar with the position of planets in the sky overhead, because they tend to show themselves very clearly just after sunset. When you get used to their position, you will notice they move a little from day to day, week to week or month to month, but there are times when the planets appear to move *backwards* for a while before resuming their usual forward motion. This apparent backward motion is caused by the fact that the Earth is also travelling around the Sun, and that all the planets are travelling at different speeds, so it can be something like being on one train that passes another one, moving in the same direction but more slowly, which makes the slower train *appear* as though it's moving backwards.

When a planet is retrograde at birth, it can cause setbacks in the person's life, and when it turns forward by transit or progression, those things should improve. Some of the people born when Mercury was retrograde find their lives are easier at those times when Mercury is retrograde by transit.

The Ancient Divisions

Planets are said to be comfortable in their own sign; for instance, Venus in Libra or Mars in Aries, but they are also comfortable when situated in their own houses, such as Mercury in the third or Jupiter in the ninth. However, there are a series of ancient placements that confer positive or negative energies. The ancient system only uses the planets that can be seen with the naked eye.

PLANET	RULERSHIP	HOUSES	EXALTATION	FALL	DETRIMENT
Sun	Leo	Fifth	Aries	Libra	Aquarius
Moon	Cancer	Fourth	Taurus	Scorpio	Capricorn
Mercury	Gemini/ Virgo	Third/ Sixth	Virgo	Pisces	Sagittarius/ Pisces
Venus	Taurus/ Libra	Second/ Seventh	Pisces	Virgo	Aries/ Scorpio
Mars	Aries/ Scorpio	First/ Eighth	Capricorn	Cancer	Taurus/ Libra
Jupiter	Sagittarius/ Pisces	Ninth/ Twelfth	Cancer	Capricorn	Gemini/ Virgo
Saturn	Capricorn/ Aquarius	Tenth/ Eleventh	Libra	Aries	Cancer/ Leo

One ancient astrologer worked out that certain degrees are actually more important than the signs as a whole, as far as exaltations are concerned. I guess the fall of each planet would be at their worst when opposing these points; so for example, Venus would be at its worst point of fall at 27 deg. Virgo.

Degrees of Exaltation

Sun	19 Aries
Moon	3 Taurus
Mercury	15 Virgo
Venus	27 Pisces
Mars	28 Capricorn
Jupiter	15 Cancer
Saturn	21 Libra

The Ruling Planet

The ruling planet is the one that rules the sign that is on the ascendant. For instance, if the chart has Cancer rising, the ruling planet is the Moon. On a chart with Scorpio rising, both Mars and Pluto should be taken into consideration. The sign and house that the ruling planet occupies are important, both natally and when affected by progressions and transits.

The Rising Planet

Some astrologers consider the rising planet to be the first after the ascendant in the first house. Others consider the rising planet to be the one that has risen over the horizon and is in the twelfth house. Most astrologers would be happy to call any planet that is near the ascendant a rising planet.

The rising planet has a bearing on the subject's early life and it can be a strong influence throughout life. For example, Saturn rising will encourage the subject to choose a profession or a lifestyle where self-discipline, a thorough knowledge of a subject, the ability to concentrate on details and to work alone is needed. According to the French statistician, Michel Gauquelin, surgeons tend to have this placement, while I have discovered that many writers also have Saturn close to the ascendant. There are many cases where there is no rising planet, because all the planets are grouped together far from the ascendant.

Mutual Reception

Two planets are in mutual reception when they are in each other's signs, such as the Moon in Taurus and Venus in Cancer. There is a strong connection between these planets and they work well together.

Unaspected Planets

In theory, unaspected planets should "disappear" from a birthchart and have a very weak impact on the subject's life, but it seems that the subject strives to develop the area that's unaspected, so it might actually become quite strong.

The Leading Planet

Some planets have a "stellium" or a bunch of planets in one area of the chart, and the first of this group is said to be the leading planet. When transits occur along the stellium, a train of events is touched off.

Midpoints

These are the halfway points between two planets, between a planet and an angle or between any two important points on a chart. These are hard to work out by hand but software does it in an instant.

Heliocentric Charts

These charts assume that we're standing on the surface of the Sun rather than the Earth. If you have decent software, you can experiment with these charts. There is a great deal missing from these charts, which makes what is left really powerful. For example, there are no houses, every chart starts at zero degrees of Aries and the Earth is placed exactly opposite to where the Sun would be on a geocentric chart, and there are no Moon and no Nodes.

Check out planets in Libra or Scorpio for relationships, Cancer and Capricorn for parents, Leo for children, Taurus for possessions and personal values and so on. Check to see whether your Earth sign represents a past life, the next life or the life you wish to have. The Earth sign may represent the Sun sign you would like to have been born with. Do the planets represent people in your life? Having tried out this method on a number of charts, I am convinced that Mars denotes the querent's father, and Mercury, the mother in a Helios chart. I have discovered that those who had diabolical childhoods and truly dreadful mothers had Mercury in Scorpio! Incidentally, all of these subjects also have enquiring minds and are hard to influence.

Chapter Three: The Personal Planets

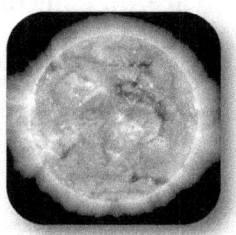

The Sun

The Sun rules the sign of Leo and the fifth house. In Roman mythology, it is associated with the god, Apollo.

The sign the Sun occupies is vitally important, because it represents all that we create and that we are. This is central to our own natures, but the creative aspect of this planet might be linked to the creation of a family, an enterprise or a lifestyle. The desire to create a happy home is a Sun matter. A decision to do something, to take action or to take an active part in anything is a Sun sign matter. The Sun is associated with success and achievement, the fun side of life, holidays, and games and gambling for fun, leisure and pleasure.

Solar Links

- The personality and general outlook on life.
- Winning, succeeding, achieving.
- Creativity in all senses of the word.
- Children.
- Fathers or father figures.
- Business, especially if it is successful or glamorous.
- Show business, glamorous professions and lifestyles.
- Entertainments, holidays, amusements, games and, to some extent, gambling and games of chance.
- Music.
- Love affairs, which are amusing diversions or deeply felt affections but they should be fun.
- Gold.

Details

The Sun is the largest and most obvious object in the sky, so it's no surprise that it exerts a very strong influence on our birthcharts. Not everyone is typical of their Sun sign, as there are many other features on a chart that have an effect. Nevertheless, the Sun is always a powerful influence.

Traditional astrology tells us that the Sun signifies the self and that it describes behaviour and character. The Sun sign determines the strength of an individual's personality and the way he chooses to live his life, his leadership qualities and his ability to exert power and authority. It can be connected with business matters.

Some older forms of astrology link the Sun to the father or father figure, and that does seem to make some sense. It is also linked with children, so either way; it is a planet that is closely related to the family as well as the self. A badly aspected natal Sun can indicate poor health, but it can also represent repression during childhood, especially by a father or father figure.

Through the association with Leo, the Sun shows how we spend our leisure time, the kind of holidays we enjoy and the things that give us pleasure. Love affairs, sporting activities, gambling, games of chance and amusements of all kinds are attributed to the Sun. Playfulness, childlike behaviour and the pursuit of fun for its own sake are also solar interests.

The Sun presides over all forms of music, entertainment and show business. Even the showbiz side of sports would come under this category. The Sun seeks success, status and pleasure from these ventures. The Sun rules anything that glistens, therefore gold and jewellery, glamorous clothes, glamorous people and fascinating, star-studded events belong to the realm of the Sun.

The Sun can be associated with successful business ventures and the creative aspect of such enterprises. A business is the manifestation of somebody's personal vision, so if the Sun shines on a business venture, it is sure to be a success.

The Moon

The Moon rules the sign of Cancer and the fourth house.

The Moon symbolises the way we feel, and this encompasses far more than just our emotional life or our personal relationships. For instance, a subject may have a job that looks good on the surface, but he may *feel* unhappy about it. The Sun acts, but the Moon reacts, and one's intuitive, reactive response is often the right one. The Moon rules our habits and our behaviour when ill, drunk or otherwise uninhibited. It represents our experience of being nurtured and our capacity to nurture others, and it is associated with the home and any property or premises that we utilise.

Lunar Links

- Inner feelings, emotions and emotional reactions, habitual behaviour and the way we are when ill, drunk or otherwise being our real selves.
- Real inner needs such as ambition, love, revenge or any other personal motivation and driving force, however well-disguised it may be.
- Mothers or mother figures, the experience of being nurtured.
- The home, premises or property and the domestic scene.
- Small shops or businesses that are run on a personal basis, often from home.
- Women, female matters.

- The public.
- Some health matters, especially chronic ones and those brought on by unhappiness.
- Travel and restlessness.
- Moods and changeability.
- Sailors and sewing (sailors were skilled at sewing sails, nets, sacks, clothing and so on).
- Dairymaids, cows.
- The cooking and storage of food, thus the larder, fridge, cooker, implements and, of course, the cook.
- Attachment to the past, patriotism, an interest in history and collecting things that have a history to them, such as antiques.
- Silver and pearls.

Details

The Moon is traditionally associated with the emotions, inner feelings, underlying urges and habitual behaviour. Ancient astrologers considered the Moon restless owing to her rapid movement through the sky, so they changeability, emotional feelings and moods to her. The Moon shows how an individual reacts to situations and how the native behaves when his passions are aroused. Some of this instinctive behaviour refers back to childhood, and it may also have some karmic significance. The underlying lunar personality will show itself when the subject is tired, ill or overwrought. It shows how a person adapts to new situations but it can also rule obsessions and deepest needs.

Traditional astrology associates the Moon with mother figures and one's first experience of being nurtured, whether, by one's own mother or by someone else. Some contemporary astrologers consider the Moon to be the childish part of a person's personality. The Moon is associated with the home, both in the sense of domestic harmony and also more practical matters, such as buying, leasing or renting property or premises. These premises may not be for living in but rather for work, renting out or keeping as a holiday home. A well-placed Moon should assure a secure and happy childhood, but the rest of the chart would need to confirm this. Even if the rest of the chart shows areas of difficulty, a comfortable Moon will be a great help to the subject.

The Moon shows the subject's attitude to the feminine, and it suggests whether or not women's issues are an important factor in a subject's life. I find it hard to reconcile the Moon's association with the idea of the public, because it seems to be so firmly tied to the private side of life, but it can show whether a person has connection with the public, serves them in any way, works with them and so on.

The Moon is not specifically associated with health but it can show up a weak area in a subject's body, along with a person's state of mind and emotional condition. Chronic ailments such as rheumatism, migraine and bronchitis can be linked to the Moon, as can cancer and feminine problems.

Earlier astrology books link the Moon with the sea and with travel and those who have the Moon in signs and houses associated with travel do seem to move around quite a lot. Early astrology books also suggested that someone with the Moon in the ninth house will marry a foreigner and that also seems to fit. I have noticed that people who have the Moon in air signs or the third, seventh or eleventh houses also travel a lot, often in connection with their work.

Mercury

Mercury rules Gemini and Virgo, the third and sixth houses of the chart. The Roman god, Mercury, was the messenger of the gods. Mercury was associated with medicine, magic and thieves!

Mercury rules thought, words, communications and knowledge. It is associated with local matters, travel, transport and movement of goods and ideas. It also concerns negotiations, paperwork and education, brothers, sisters and neighbours. A fair amount of the things we all do as part of normal daily life are associated with Mercury.

Mercury Links

- Communications.
- Travel and transport.
- Local matters, the neighbourhood.
- Knowledge.
- Primary and secondary education.
- The mind, the mental processes, the way one thinks.
- Brothers and sisters, cousins and similar relationships.
- Youthfulness.
- Health and healing.
- Magic.
- Sales and marketing.
- Thieves and theft.
- Rail and bus termini.
- Boundary markers.
- Cinnabar, mercury.

Details

Mercury rules all forms of communication, such as speech, thought, writing and messages, including those that travel though the body's nervous system. In modern life, Mercury is associated with communication gadgets of all kinds.

Mercury traditionally rules local travel and transport, but the world is so small now that it can be linked to slightly more distant travel. Post, emails and much else related to communications comes under the rule of Mercury. Mercury rules sales, marketing, and many activities associated with business.

Anything that requires skill is typically Mercurial; therefore, craftwork, light engineering, dressmaking and the use of office machinery come into this category. Mercury signifies knowledge, teaching and learning.

Traditional astrology suggests that Mercury rules primary, secondary and further education while Jupiter rules higher education. Languages are particularly Mercurial, as is computer programming. Mercury rules the mind, the ability to think on one's feet and to cope with everyday life. Dyslexia tends to show up when Mercury is retrograde and close to the ascendant.

Mercury rules the locality, neighbours, local shops, schools and anything else that is nearby or places that the subject visits on a frequent basis. Well-placed Mercury suggests living in a friendly area with good local facilities and a happy environment, while badly-aspected Mercury could bring difficult neighbours and an unpleasant neighbourhood.

This planet is associated with brothers, sisters and cousins or other relatives of one's own age, along with close relationships, especially if the friends live nearby. It's also linked to young people and all the things they love to do. Mercurial types stay young at heart even when they get old.

Mercury is concerned with health and healing, especially when the hands are used to diagnose or to heal. The Roman symbol for this god was the caduceus or herald's wand, and this is still used as a healing symbol today. This may be why Mercury is also linked to magic, shamanism and so forth, as there can be positive aspects to healing but it can also be open to charlatanism.

Mercury also rules trickery and sharp practice, along with an element both of concealment and revelation because this planet is the link between this world and the next. He seems to know more than he is prepared to reveal to us and therefore is both wiser and trickier than we realise.

Venus

Venus rules Taurus and Libra, and the second and seventh houses. Venus was the Roman goddess of love.

Venus is associated with the things we hold dear to us, which includes material possessions, land and our values and priorities. Venus is concerned with anything that appeals to the senses, which includes music and art, dancing, food, sex, fresh air and anything else that feels good and does us good. We can be very attached to the things that we own or enjoy, so Venus shows what we will fight to keep. It also rules our image. Venus rules relationships that are open to scrutiny, which may mean a husband or a close associate but it can just as easily concern an open and acknowledged enemy.

Venus Links

- Values and priorities.
- Valuable goods and personal possessions.
- Personal finances.
- Love, romance and sexuality.
- Leisure and pleasure.
- Music and art.
- Ostentation and luxury.
- Females.
- Emotions connected to love and possessions.
- Open friendships and relationships such as marriage.
- Open enemies and the reason for fighting.
- Mirrors, decorative glass, Venetian blinds.

- Cosmetics, powder compacts (with and without mirrors).
- Sea shells, flowers, oysters.
- Aphrodisiacs and venereal diseases (although AIDS comes under the rulership of Pluto).
- Copper, malachite and emeralds.
- Justice and fair play.
- Legal arguments.
- Balance, harmony.

Details

Venus is associated with the things one values, especially our own personal goods and personal finances, but it also relates to things we value, such as time to oneself, time to do something other than work and of valuing something other than material goods. An important aspect of this is self-value and self-esteem.

Venus was the Roman goddess of love. We tend to see this nowadays as romantic love, but the Romans saw Venus as a sexual being and the temple maidens who were dedicated to her were very far from being Vestal Virgins! Venusian love puts the loved one on a pedestal, but it can also signify greed, possessiveness and jealousy. Don't forget the idea of ownership that is associated with this planet. In some cases, a partner can be seen as a meal ticket or a status symbol. Pets can be loved to distraction but they are also a form of possession.

Venus is associated with leisure and pleasure, also with singing, playing an instrument and with music. Sometimes Venus can go over the top and sink into hedonism, drunkenness, self-indulgence and a love of luxury. All sorts of surprisingly deep emotions are wrapped up with this planet, such as a need for comfort and safety but also envy, jealousy and possessiveness and sentimentality. Venus signifies relationships that are open and above board, so it rules love partnerships, business partnerships and close associations of all kinds, but it is also concerned with open enemies.

The position of Venus can give some clue as to whether or not the subject will ever have children. When activated by progression or transit, it can indicate birth, with female children being more likely than male ones. Be careful when dealing with this because you may give someone who can't have children false hopes.

Venus rules anything that appeals to the senses, so this applies to nice food, perfume, a beautiful garden or a lovely house, music, dancing, singing, art, culture, colour, shape, fashion or anything else which we enjoy.

Venus denotes the feminine principle and is associated with all that is soft and feminine within every one of us but paradoxically Venus is too materialistic to make sacrifices for others. This planet represents the beauty and sexual attractiveness of women. Venus in a man's chart can suggest the kind of woman who would interest him.

Venus is also concerned with justice, balance and harmony, and she will go openly into battle against an injustice if necessary. Venus rules arbitration, adjudication, marriage counselling, family counselling and brokering of any kind, which brings an attachment to the law, especially where it specialises in settling financial or family arguments.

Mars

Mars rules Aries and before the discovery of Pluto, it was also assigned to the sign of Scorpio. It rules the first house and was once also the ruler of the eighth house. Mars was, of course, the Roman god of war.

Mars rules energy and drive. On one hand, Mars adds assertiveness, courage and sexuality but it can add aggression, violence and danger. Too much Mars is much like too much adrenalin or testosterone, while the right amount gives a subject the heart to fight when the need is there. This planet is not concerned with actual possessions and material objects but it can show how these are acquired.

Mars Links

- Energy, assertiveness, forcefulness, initiative, etc.
- Passion, the desire for something.
- The drive to obtain the person or the object of one's desire.
- Decision-making and decisive action.
- Arguments and violence.
- Masculine occupations such as engineering steel making and (with Pluto) coal mining.
- Competitive activities, especially sports.
- Iron and steel, surgical instruments.
- Tools, especially knives, blades.
- Warfare, weapons, the tools of destruction.
- Blood.
- Iron.

Details

Mars is associated with energy, force, drive, courage and the masculine side within all of us. This planet represents the macho aspect of the personality, and without Mars somewhere on our charts, nobody would ever get up out of bed to do anything! A subject with a strong Mars is assertive, energetic and courageous, but if the Mars energy is overdone, the subject will be hot tempered, apt to leap before he looks and possibly even violent or self-destructive.

Mars relates to masculine activities, such as car maintenance and engineering, along with the tools that are used in these activities, especially metal ones. It can have some connection with explosives, especially those used for an engineering purpose. The red planet concerns driving at speed and all kind of sports, especially team games and fast or dangerous sports, along with the armed services, the police, the fire service and paramedics, or any other job that requires courage and the wearing of a special uniform. It rules courage and perseverance in the face of major obstacles.

This planet rules the masculine aspect of sexuality and one's sex drive. It also suggests the kind of man who a woman finds attractive. For instance, I've known women with Mars in Aries or Scorpio who are attracted to men in uniforms and men who do what we would consider particularly masculine jobs.

Chapter Four: The Transpersonal Planets

Jupiter

Jupiter was the king of the Roman gods, and he could be very generous and philanthropic, but also angry and destructive. Jupiter rules the sign of Sagittarius and the ninth house. Before the discovery of Neptune, Jupiter was also associated with the sign of Pisces and the twelfth house. Jupiter is a transpersonal planet, so it is less concerned with a subject's actions and feelings than with the person's experiences life in general. Jupiter signifies expansion, exploration and anything that pushes back boundaries, surmounts barriers and creates opportunities. The general idea is to take a concept, a desire or an opportunity and run with it as far as you can go, although Jupiter can destroy some things to make room for something better

Jupiter Links

- Foreign travel or exploration of new places.
- The law and the legal system.
- Belief, religion and philosophy.
- What you believe in and feel strongly about.
- Education, especially higher education.
- Business and success.
- Opportunities.
- Meeting new and influential people.
- Publishing and broadcasting.
- Large animals.
- Outdoor life and sporting activities.
- Gambling and winning – traditionally, gambling on horses.
- Tin.

Details

Jupiter expands the native's horizons in several different ways, these being higher education, religion and philosophy, the law and travel or overseas exploration. The notion of exploration and expansion in connection with foreign travel is obvious but it is also inherent in the other Jupiterian concepts.

Education expands an individual's knowledge and understanding, and because Jupiter is concerned with higher education, this allows the person to explore an idea or area of knowledge much further than basic schooling can achieve. Jupiter takes the time to think, to dream and to explore widely. Nobody finds religion, philosophy, belief or propaganda interesting unless he thinks about these things. Depth of knowledge and understanding characterise education and religion, but sadly, certain religious beliefs engender fear, hatred and intolerance, which are the darker side of the old Roman god's nature.

Legal matters require specialist help and advice. In the past solicitors administered land, inheritances and money matters and to some extent, they still do, but the complications of taxation and modem business mean that accountancy has now become a separate field, but this too is Jupiterian, as it is the legal aspect of this that works here, while business itself is assigned to Capricorn. The law may not seem to link to exploration but lawyers test ideas and people and they push against the boundaries. The law can be used to protect the populace or to repress it, a fact that once again illustrates the dark side of Jove.

Jupiter is associated with publishing and also with broadcasting, which are ways of getting one's words and one's ideas "out there". It is linked to tolerance and acceptance of ethnic and racial differences and of being interested in new or different ways of thinking. It's also associated with large animals, and thus to horse racing and gambling. It is a planet of glamour; grandeur and a life lived to the full. Other Jupiterian concepts include sports and competitive activities, although in the sense of competition for the fun of it rather than serious dedication. Jupiter is linked to a sense of humour and enjoyment of life. There is a lucky aspect to this planet as it can bring opportunity and change for the better. It also brings meetings with new people, growth and depth to an enterprise. However, Jupiter was known for tossing down thunderbolts from time to time, so it can bring problems in its wake.

Saturn

Saturn is the second and last transpersonal planet, and it rules Capricorn and the tenth house. Before Uranus was discovered, Saturn also ruled Aquarius and the eleventh house. Saturn was the Roman god of time and of old age.

Saturn helps us reach our goals and see the rewards for our efforts, but he also rules difficult circumstances and times of restriction or limitation. This planet presides over foundations, craftsmanship and attention to detail and ultimate success through hard work and persistence, so it can rule long-winded tasks.

Saturn sets boundaries and it shows where and how we may be limited by circumstances. Saturn should not be considered as an enemy but a means of learning and developing and of giving us the character and backbone that we need in order to get through life.

Saturn Links

- Endurance, persistence, restraint and caution.
- Self-discipline, organisation, knowing the right time to do something.
- Ambition, success that is well deserved.
- Maturity, senior citizenship, old age.
- Some aspects of pain and suffering, especially if the situation is lasting or chronic.
- Banking, big business, large organisations.
- Structure and a firm foundation.
- Authority and status.

- Lead, pipes - especially household plumbing, and of course, plumbers.
- Clocks, watches and timepieces of all kinds.
- Measuring instruments of all kinds, such as rulers, weights, slide rules, computers used for mathematical purposes.
- Calculations and in ancient times, astrology.
- Coffin makers.
- Masonry, building materials, the building trade.
- Taboos.

Details

Saturn rules structure, foundations and work that are carried out in an orderly, structured and disciplined manner. Anything that we do thoroughly is Saturnian, so this planet rules craftsmanship, attention to detail and finishing what one starts. Saturn is connected to responsibilities, obligations and the idea of getting the work done before we can rush off and have a good time. We respect the type of person who works hard, and despise the one who walks away from responsibilities or refuses to put himself out to help others. Too much Saturn can result is a person spending his life under the control of others, but he may cope with this situation by enduring it, because endurance is another Saturnian concept.

A well-placed Saturn, along with other pleasant factors on a chart suggests that this person had a childhood in which he experienced encouragement and reasonable discipline along with love, security and proper care. His parents fed him well, ensured that he had a nice room and a warm and comfortable bed, decent friends and guardians, good school attendance and so on. Saturn rules team games, joint efforts and the family pulling together in order to achieve something worthwhile.

As far as material concepts are concerned, Saturn rules banking, big business, large structures and organisations, trees, wood and probably the earth itself, along with lead and radiation shields. It also rules heaviness in all its forms ranging from a heavy object to a heavy heart! Saturn is considered to be the ruler of old age and things that are worth working for or waiting for, such as well-deserved feeling of success, increased status, wealth, an organised kitchen, a royalty payment or a myriad other well-earned blessings. It rules serious people who have real knowledge and are therefore, worthy of our respect.

There are some really unpleasant concepts that come under the realm of Saturn, such as crippling shyness, self-doubt, low self-esteem, self-hatred, severe embarrassment, a blow to the ego, and also suffering and loss. Also, chronic illness and disability, but, before you slide back into the habit of blaming Saturn for every ill, please remember that all the planets have a downside.

Chapter Five: The Impersonal Planets

Uranus

According to mythology, Uranus was the god of the stormy heavens, and he was the son of the earth goddess, Gaia. Saturn castrated him and threw his genitals into the sea, upon which the foaming stormy mess of blood and semen bubbled and boiled and eventually gave birth to Venus.

Uranus is the first of the outer planets, which are known in astrology as the impersonal planets. These planets take several years to move through each sign, so they represent a particular era. Uranus is considered to be the planet of change, of revolution, rebellion and refusal to conform. It's concerned with ideas rather than feelings, and it's especially associated with group and political activities, so it relates to original thinking, new inventions and fresh ideas.

Uranian people like to consider themselves "different", and they may have a point, because their planet certainly is different from all the others: it revolves in the opposite direction to all the other planets. It's also the coldest of all the planets.

Uranus Links

- Groups and political activities, especially green or humanitarian ones.
- Idealism, humanitarianism, any other 'ism' that supposedly benefits the group as a whole.
- Individualism, independence, self-motivation.
- Ideas, concepts.
- Technical innovation and inventions that may change the world.
- Originality.
- Shocks and surprises - some nice, some nasty, but all enlightening.
- Obstinacy and eccentricity.
- Uranium.

Details

In the 1960s and early 1970s when I was learning astrology, much was made of the totalitarian nature of Uranus which was due to usher in the age of Big Brother and the thought police, because Uranian ideas were considered to be utilitarian, devoted to equality and the submergence of individual feelings, desires and needs. Nowadays, Uranus is associated with quirky individualism, a desire for freedom and independence and with all people being equal. Uranus rules group activities and organisations, which may range from racist or militant religions, to "green" organisations, trades unions, new political parties and issues, along with gentler kinds of clubs, societies and community centres geared to the needs of particular groups of people.

Uranus rules friendship and acquaintanceship rather than close personal relationships. It relates to the need to learn for oneself and to find out the hard way. Uranus is associated with education in all its forms it wants to see ideas and knowledge being spread as far and as widely as possible. It's particularly linked to educational organisations and groups.

Uranus can signify obstinacy and the determination to get things done. It is unconventional and original in it's thinking, and it links to flashes of intuition, genius, clairvoyance, sudden shocks and life-changing events. It denotes science fact and science fiction and the kind of imagination that produces both of these, and almost anything else which is weird and different. Uranian people are so individual that they aren't even like other Uranian people. They march to their own drumbeat and don't follow the herd. Many Uranian people have strong feelings about some cause or other, such as the needs of animals, education, religion or politics. It's a waste of time trying to argue with a Uranian type. They consider themselves hugely logical and open minded, but they are devoted to their own opinions and they can't be influenced – not even when common sense stares them in the face.

Neptune

In mythology, Neptune was the god of the sea, and the cause of earthquakes. This planet is something of a misnomer in astrology, because its attributes have more to do with the god Morpheus than with Neptune, except for the odd fact that two of Neptune's moons are Oberon and Titania, who were the god and goddess of dreams, in addition to being the King and Queen of the fairies. In astrology, Neptune rules Pisces and the twelfth house.

Neptune rules the highest that we can aspire to and the lowest levels of degradation. It brings confusion, but also revelation, self-delusion but also compassion and pure love. This planet presides over the creation of illusion for entertainment in films, television and music, also illusions brought on by strange moods, alcohol and drugs.

Neptune Links

- Illusions, both good and bad kinds.
- Appreciation of things other than the basic needs of food, clothing and shelter.
- Love of God and religious or mystical revelations.
- Romantic love, especially when one endows the lover with virtues that he or she doesn't actually have.
- Creativity, especially if the creation depends upon illusion, as in film.
- Shifting sands, nothing being what it seems.
- Lies, deception and self-deception.
- The sea and fishing.

- Travel to or over water.
- Holidays on or by water or snow.
- Gas, smells, perfume, anaesthetics.
- Alcohol and drugs.
- Glass, especially when used in a functional rather than in a decorative manner, such as for windows or spectacles, microscopes, telescopes and so on.
- Photography and film.
- Self-sacrifice, social work, doing things for others.
- Places of seclusion such as hospitals, prisons and mental institutions.
- The workers and the work that is associated with these places.
- Voluntary workers.

Details

Neptune rules concepts that are hard to describe, such as inspiration, imagination, illusion and delusion. The planet rules the appreciation of those things that are beyond the basic needs of food, clothing and shelter, so it presides over artistry, music, film and television programmes.

Neptune brings truth, light and wisdom but it also causes muddles and confusion, and it causes us to lose our way. This planet is associated with kindness, pity, charity and love but these concepts can all too easily be twisted and misused. Many ordinary people give freely to the starving people in Somalia, Ethiopia and the Sudan only to discover that the goods they have bought have been hi-jacked and used to feed warlords and their armies or to pay for their armaments. Mysticism, religious inspiration and a life dedicated to doing God's work, but also to fanaticism and religious intolerance. This planet is associated with the sea, fish and fishing, which give it a powerful link to Christianity.

Neptune denotes escape from the world and sometimes to confinement. This can be due to a spell in hospital, prison or simply staying at home. It rules orphanages, asylums, hospitals, prisons and hospices or any other place where people are confined either for their own good or for the good of society. This planet is also connected to religious retreats, enclosed orders and any other means of escape or of retreat from the world. It is linked to charity and self-less giving.

Neptune is especially associated with escape from normal life by means of alcohol and drugs. This planet can lead to deceptions, lies and swindles, along with muddles, mistakes and things that go missing. When someone falls in love, he is confused, unable to think straight and he may be unable to eat, sleep and function normally for a while. Unrequited love is particularly Neptunian, as is the kind of love that blinds an individual to the truth.

Neptune is associated with hypnotherapy and altered states of consciousness, with joy and ecstasy and with gloom and depression. It can lead one to see others through rose coloured glasses or to see them as the enemy when they are not.

Pluto

In Roman mythology, Pluto was the hugely wealthy king of the underworld, and in astrology, it rules Scorpio and the eighth house. Astronomers have recently demoted Pluto to a dwarf planet, and it certainly is a small object, compared to others but it has a profound effect in astrology.

Pluto is associated with transformation, commitment but also with deeply held resentment and hatred. It rules partnerships, joint financial arrangements and important financial matters, particularly where other people are involved. It presides over things that are hidden from the eye and the means of uncovering or extracting these. Most of all it symbolises transformation and the collective unconscious.

Pluto rules the deeper and more difficult aspects of our lives and with transforming events, up to and including birth and death. It changes people and circumstances on a deep and profound level, but on a lighter note, it rules recycling, having a clear out and transforming our lives for the better. It is linked with shared resources and with financial dealings, especially those that crop up at times of great change, such as the joining of one's resources when forming a partnership or dealing with banks, legacies, business finances and other people's money or goods.

Pluto Links

- Birth and death.
- The passage to the "other side".

- Transformation, recycling, changing from one state to another.
- Sex, procreation and committed relationships.
- Wills, legacies, taxes, accountancy on behalf of others.
- Business matters related to money, stocks and shares, insurance.
- Business commitments.
- Mining, excavation, archaeology.
- Butchery, surgery, cutting with knives.
- Psychiatry, unlocking the unconscious.
- Investigation, espionage, counter espionage.
- Engineering, military matters, macho images.
- Power broking, power behind the scenes, manipulation.

Details

Pluto is associated with wills, legacies and corporate matters. It may not rule business as such but the act of becoming involved in a business or changes that occur within that business are linked to Pluto. This planet rules taxes and bills, bank accounts, the stock market and shares, pensions and insurance, especially life insurance and the administration of other people's finances.

Pluto rules procreation, both in the sense of bringing a new life into the world as well as the birth of an enterprise or an idea. Pluto also rules sex, sexual scandals and sexual indiscretions, but on the other hand, Pluto is also concerned with committed relationships and married love.

Pluto rules mining and the act of digging out things that are buried, such as gold, diamonds, oil and coal. It also rules bank vaults and archaeology. This planet relates to all that is covert, such as spies and spying, but also the police, investigation, intelligence, military matters and atomic weapons.

Pluto signifies power games and manipulative behaviour and those who act as the power behind the throne. It also rules psychiatry and the ability to get to the bottom of things, such as hidden motives and corrosive resentments. Some health problems are Plutonic, especially those that affect the lower spine, reproductive organs or things that can't easily be seen or got at. Surgery is linked to Pluto because it cuts through to what is inside. Pluto is concerned with butchery and engineering. Pluto is far from being bad, because everything has to be recycled one way or another, including life itself.

Chiron

In mythology, Chiron was the king of the centaurs and the teacher of heroes, including Hercules, Jason and Perseus. He was accidentally shot in the heel by one of Hercules' poisoned arrows and the wound festered. Chiron couldn't be cured, but being immortal, he couldn't die either, so he suffered terribly until he exchanged his immortality with Prometheus, who had lost his. It interesting to note that, before his accident, Chiron was known as the greatest of the healers. His daughter, Manta, was said to have invented astrology and the other mantic arts.

Chiron is a dwarf planet that is associated with sickness that comes on suddenly, accidents that lead to pain and suffering, along with physical, mental and emotional pain and chronic ailments. It's also associated with healing of all kinds. There is a slight link with teaching and with martial arts. There is no definite rule, but I have always associated Chiron with the sign of Virgo and the sixth house.

Chiron links:

- Illness, accidents and pain.
- Emotional and psychological damage.
- Healing of all kinds.
- Slight attachment to learning combat techniques.
- Slight attachment to learning music.

Details

A strong Chiron in a birthchart denotes a subject who wishes to work in medicine, teaching or counselling, possibly due to a desire to alleviate suffering or to encourage others to make something of themselves. It is said to represent the area of hurt in our charts, and this may be a practical health problem or a psychological one.

It seems to have the greatest influence when it is close to the angles or in angular houses, such as the fourth and tenth houses for difficult relationships with parents, or close to the ascendant or descendant for personal problems or difficulties in love relationships.

Chapter Six: Other Features on a Chart

The Asteroid - Vesta

Vesta rules the comfort and cosiness of a nice home and a good family. It also seems to show the kind of home life we come from or that we choose to have. The Romans believed that bad behaviour would bring Vesta down on one's head in the form of karmic retribution.

The Asteroid - Ceres

Ceres rules the harvest and cereals, and thus symbolically comfort and abundance.

The Nodes of the Moon

When the Moon crosses the ecliptic in an upward direction, the crossing point is called the North Node of that planet and the southward crossing point becomes the South Node.

The North Node of the Moon

- Your present and future karma.

- How you fit into current social and political thinking.
- Some astrologers see this as a lucky point, others as the opposite.
- Good luck with matters related to the family, property and premises.

The South Node of the Moon

- Your past karma and your past life.
- How your desires differ from 'political correctness' or from the society in which you live.
- Difficulty in getting things off the ground.
- Some astrologers see this as a lucky point, others as the opposite.

Details

There are three ways of looking at the Nodes of the Moon, starting with an idea taken from Hindu astrology, which says that the Nodes are connected to karma and reincarnation. Indian astrologers refer to the North Node as the dragon's head (Rahu) and the South Node as the dragon's tail (Kethu), and they consider the dragon itself to be a pretty evil influence.

The idea is that the South Node represents our previous lives and those things that we have already learned or overcome, but we struggle to come to terms with the lessons of our current life, as represented by the North Node. The Moon itself has a connection with the past, so previous experiences and past-life experiences do seem to have relevance when looking at the Nodes.

Western astrologers see the North Node as an area on our charts where we are attuned to the current outlook that prevails in society, while the South Node might put us against the general trend and make us seem rebellious and out of tune with the views of others. A common effect is something related to property or premises. Minor transits to the Nodes indicate trivial events such as going on holiday, having visitors or decorating and renovating the home.

If you look at the transits of the Nodes in the ephemeris, in addition to looking at progressions and transits of other planets to your own Nodes, you will be surprised at how important they can be.

The Angles

The Ascendant is on the left of the chart, and it marks the start of the first house. It's usually abbreviated as Asc. It rules the following concepts:

- Childhood programming.
- Outer manner, and thus the way others see you.
- Some aspects of the body and health.

The Descendant is opposite the Ascendant on the chart, and it marks the start of the seventh house. It's usually expressed as Dsc. It is linked with the following items:

- The kind of people we attract.
- What we enjoy in others.
- Some aspects of partners and friends.

At the top is the Midheaven or Medium Coeli, which is usually expressed as the MC, and it marks the start of the tenth house in most house systems. It is associated with the following:

- Where we are trying to get to in this life.
- Aims and aspirations.
- Career or where you would like to be in life.
- What you would like to achieve.
- Some aspects of partners and friends.

- Where you are headed.
- Father figures or paternal role models.
- Authority figures.

The bottom is the Nadir or Immum Coeli, and it marks the start of the fourth house in most house systems. It is known as the IC and it links to the following ideas:

- The family background and collective unconscious.
- What the family wanted the subject to be.
- Mother figures and maternal role models.
- Nurturing figures.
- Where the person is coming from, so to speak.

Sensitive Points

There are many of these, but here are two that you might like to experiment with:

- **The Vertex** rules important events that occur via other people, and the most obvious ones are falling in love or bereavement, but there are many other less dramatic ones.
- **The Part of Fortune** comes from an Arabic system of astrology and it shows how you get ahead in life and even how you might make your fortune.

Chapter Seven: The Sun through the Signs

The Sun in Aries

Aries is a masculine, cardinal, fire sign, ruled by Mars.

Arians are energetic, enterprising, outgoing and competitive and they can be impulsive, so a typical Arian won't let the grass grow under his feet but he is impatient with details, easily bored and needs to be busy both at work and socially. Arians like to be part of a large organisation with a set structure and a ladder to climb, but if they work for themselves, they will find a way of joining up with others or of leading a team. Somewhat impulsive and always optimistic, Arians look forward with faith in the future and they don't usually bear grudges. These subjects are kind hearted and very good to their friends and family, they are generous, helpful and very good hosts or hostesses. Arians are competitive and they like to be the best of the bunch, but can lack the persistence. Aries women need a career outside the home, and both men and women often have hobbies in addition to demanding careers. These subjects cannot sit about for long and they are not great television viewers because they become restless and easily bored.

They make loving parents and while they may push their children a bit too much, they will do anything they can to help them. Arians surprisingly home loving and most are not actually keen on too much travel. Most appreciate art, beauty, poetry and music and they have an excellent sense of humour. Arians have a surprisingly spiritual side to them that attracts them to religion or a spiritual way of thinking. A surprising number of them are drawn to psychic matters, and their intuition and keen interest in spiritual life can make them excellent clairvoyants and psychic mediums.

The Sun in Taurus

Taurus is a feminine, fixed, earth sign, ruled by Venus.

Taureans are practical, patient, thorough, tenacious and reliable. The Sun in Taurus acts in a slow and patient manner and it has a common sense attitude. The creativity of the Sun is expressed in something solid, such as a building project, landscape gardening, dancing, cookery or singing. The chief fault of this sign is stubbornness or to drop whatever hobbyhorse they climb on.

Taureans need to feel secure and to have a well-filled bank account behind them. These subjects are close to their families and loyal to their friends but if they take a dislike to someone, they make implacable enemies. They may irritate their partners or their children by wanting to know exactly where they are going and what time they are coming home. These dexterous people often find work in artistic or creative fields and many of them make inspired builders, decorators, hairdressers and make-up artists. Taurean people are extremely sociable, so they love to meet new people and to be out and about at all kinds of function. They love holidays with their family and friends, but if they go alone or with a partner, they soon make new friends. They just love strolling around in the sunshine. These people are usually pleasant, ordinary, reliable and shrewd. They can sometimes be taken for fools, but they can use that to their advantage on occasion.

Some choose to wear weird and wonderful clothing, either to amuse people when at a function or because they simply enjoy dressing differently. Some like to shock people, and some can be quite offensive. Most are reliable workers but they don't like to be rushed, so they keep going at their own pace.

The Sun in Gemini

*Gemini is a masculine, mutable, air sign,
ruled by Mercury.*

Gemini is flexible in its approach, changeable and sometimes intellectual. The Sun here expresses itself by taking in information and then releasing it again. Gemini people can live and work alone, but draw people towards them, so their phone is rarely at rest. Gemini subjects are astute but they may hop from one subject to another without studying anything too deeply. However, if their interest is aroused, they can get into something to a greater depth.

These subjects are loyal to their families and they care deeply for their children, and while they don't like too many changes in their relationships, like all air signs, they can drift in and out of friendships as the mood takes them. These excellent communicators often work in jobs that keep them in touch with others, which is why so many of them work in the media. Many Geminis are attracted to figure-work so they find jobs in banking and accountancy.

Geminis enjoy travel and sports but they are not particularly strong, so they need to conserve their easily depleted physical energies. These subjects are more sensible and hard-working than they are given credit for, and they can be determined when they set their sights on something. Geminis are good homemakers but they need the stimulus of a decent job or a strong outside interest. They also appreciate having money to spend and they are happy to earn it. Geminis need personal freedom and they hate being questioned about their comings and goings. Their main downside is a tendency to become depressed.

The Sun in Cancer

Cancer is a feminine, cardinal, water sign, ruled by the Moon.

Cardinal signs like to make their own decisions, while the water element brings emotion, intuition and sensitivity. Their combination of shrewdness, common sense and intuition makes them excellent sales people who have a sure touch with the public.

Cancerians do well in any job that deals with the public, because they have an instinctive feel for what people need, and they provide this with charm and efficiency. They can calm those who are angry or hysterical without becoming infected with anger themselves, assuming this situation occurs in a business or working environment and not inside their own homes and families. They tend to fall apart when the going gets rough at home. They do best when they ally themselves either to a calm and resilient partner or to an adventurous one. Cancerians enjoy family life and they often work with family members. Cancerians are sensitive and easily hurt but they learn to hide their sensitivity under a hard shell and, in some cases over a period of time, the soft heart atrophies, making them unfeeling to the point of cruelty.

Cancer is careful with money, so they usually save and avoid getting into debt. Many Cancerians love to travel and while they need the security of a home base, they love getting away from it to explore new places.

The Sun in Leo

Leo is a masculine, fixed, fire sign, ruled by the Sun.

Leos are playful in nature so they like their lives to have an element in fun in them. These people are successful, glamorous and popular but they can be stubborn, determined and arrogant. Leo people are proud and their standards are high. These people are not materialistic in the sense of needing a large pile of savings in the bank or of wanting to have more than the Joneses, but they want everything life can offer. They want to succeed and they want their families to be happy and successful.

Leos are usually kind and generous, good natured and sociable but they can become mean and cranky if life doesn't go their way. These subjects can be restless, impatient and critical but they are often harder on themselves than they are on others. Leos have old-fashioned values, being basically honest, hard-working family people.

These subjects need an adventurous life and a prestigious or glamorous line of work, but they will stick to a poor job if necessary. Leos often choose jobs that allow them to travel or to get out and about and talk to people. Leos are not usually intellectual or academic, so their thinking is slow and rather inflexible and their ideas and interests quite mundane. One of their greatest assets is their organisational talents and their sheer ability to get things done. Leos are not as dramatic or as outgoing as most astrologers seem to think, because they are easily embarrassed and they don't like to make a spectacle of themselves. Their kindness and sympathy can make them a soft touch for less scrupulous people.

The Sun in Virgo

*Virgo is a feminine, mutable, earth sign,
ruled by Mercury; also, arguably, by Chiron.*

Virgos are concerned with detail and they make good database managers, record keepers and bookkeepers, but they don't catch on to new ideas too quickly. They are modest and sometimes fussy. The earth element signifies that they do things thoroughly and they don't like to be rushed. They make good editors and journalists, and many are into cooking or needlework, farming or draughtsmanship.

Their standards are very high and they blame themselves when things go wrong. They are sensitive and easily hurt, but also critical of others. They have a reputation for tidiness but they are no more tidy or untidy than any other sign, but they do get annoyed if others tidy up their stuff for them. Virgos are careful and discriminating, and they have a talent for analysis. They may have some special are of knowledge, but they also have a good range of general knowledge.

Some Virgoans have strangely split personalities, being extremely modest and retiring in some situations, and outgoing in others. Some are defensive and difficult, while other Virgos are the salt of the earth, being kind, gentle and witty, with delightful senses of humour and hearts of gold. The nicest Virgoans are drawn to work in fields where they can help others. Their worst fault is a tendency to shoot themselves in the foot and ruin things for themselves. Virgos are very good to their parents and other relatives and they don't usually let others down.

The Sun in Libra

Libra is a masculine, cardinal, air sign, ruled by Venus.

Libra is concerned with balance, harmony and fair play but it is also quite a tough and adventurous sign. The Sun in Libra expresses itself in a co-operative manner, and any enterprise is carried out in as pleasant and charming a way as possible. Librans have a deceptive appearance, because they are good looking and they can look soft and gentle, but they have a tough core that allows them to cope with difficult situations.

Librans can be very persuasive, so they make wonderful agents and they make excellent diplomats, lawyers and negotiators. Librans can't take too much stress so they need a reliable career and good relationships, but they are more ambitious than they appear. There are some strange polarities with this sign, as some are extremely clean and tidy, while others are the opposite. Similarly, some are extremely well organised and hard working, while others are the exact opposite. As you can see, this sign can run to extremes. Some Librans have a problem with decision-making, while others just need time to come to their conclusions. The reason for this shilly-shallying is their finely balanced legal minds, which tend to look at all sides of a question and to examine the rightness of their choices, along with a preference for stopping and thinking before committing themselves.

These subjects are very flirtatious, and some of them have a real problem with fidelity. Some prefer to keep their options open and to explore a variety of relationships. Librans are cheerful, optimistic, humorous, good-natured and loving, but they can be sharp tongued and cruel when the mood hits them. Boredom is their worst enemy. Librans are wonderful company and great talkers and they have the knack of understanding other people. Many Librans tend to live in cloud cuckoo land sometimes rather than to face reality.

The Sun in Scorpio

Scorpio is a feminine, fixed, water sign,
ruled by Pluto and, in older traditions, Mars.

There is a resilience and determination about this sign that makes them able to live through difficult times and to cope with hardship in ways that would poleaxe others. These people are the workers of the zodiac who like to turn up on time, do a good job and to finish what they start. Their motto is "if you are going do to something, do it properly!" The go at things with great energy and enthusiasm and once they start something they stick with it until the end. Scorpios are reliable, resourceful, hard working and intensely loyal. They are well organised and they have good memories. They are excellent salespeople because they have the tenacity and determination to see things through. They expect others to be as thorough and as capable as they are though, and they can show contempt for those who aren't. Scorpios prefer to be the second in command than to lead an organisation. They make good marriage partners but they are moody and they don't always tell their partners what is on their minds. If Scorpios have problems at work or in a social setting, they may release their tensions by behaving badly to their loved ones.

Most are charming and likeable, and they genuinely love to help others. Their tough appearance and manner often hides a kind and generous heart, although some Scorpios actually relate better to animals than to people. They make wonderful friends and they can be the most loyal and dependable partners. Their feelings are very deep and they don't forgive those who hurt them. Some have a fear of abandonment, while others tend to worry over small things. These inexplicable feelings may be carried forward from childhood experiences or even a previous life. Being an all or nothing sign, some are very generous while others are very tight fisted, while some drink too much and others barely drink at all. They can be romantic and very loving.

The Sun in Sagittarius

Sagittarius is a masculine, mutable, fire sign,
ruled by Jupiter.

People born under Sagittarius usually fall on their feet. These people are pleasant, cheerful and optimistic, but their intense honesty can make them tactless and outspoken.

Astrology books tell us that Sagittarians live very exciting lives, travelling, exploring and making new friends wherever they go, but many prefer to plod along with a secure home life and nothing to rock the boat.

They are artistic and creative and many are very capable, especially when it comes to building work or do-in-yourself. These subjects enjoy working for large organisations where they can meet a variety of people, and they are good at dealing with the public or with people who have problems. They make excellent teachers and are often happiest in that line of work. There is a common belief that all Sagittarians love horses but the reality is that they are like the rest of us, in that they may enjoy having a dog or a cat as a pet, but that's about all.

Some of these individuals are rather rebellious in childhood while others reject parental affection, but many have poor childhoods with fathers who abandon the family and mothers who find it hard to cope. Both sexes are generous with their time and some are also generous with money and goods, so they can lay themselves open to being used or taken advantage of. If they are hurt or let down, they don't forgive or forget. They aren't prejudiced on the grounds of race or religion - indeed, they fight against such prejudice. Sagittarians can be great fighters for justice and fair play, and their strong social conscience can lead them to work in the law or the Church. They are often into spirituality, religion, New Age thinking or psychism. They question the religion they were brought up with and find their own way later in life.

The Sun in Capricorn

Capricorn is a feminine, cardinal, earth sign,
ruled by Saturn.

The Sun expresses itself in a steady and thorough manner in Capricorn. Capricorn folks are patient, realistic, respectable, responsible and hard working. They don't walk away from unpalatable situations lightly and they stick to marriages and partnerships as long as possible. However, this is a cardinal sign, not a fixed one, which means that they won't put up with something unnecessarily. Capricorns are refined and gentle, so they dislike rough or crude people. Most of all, they hate to be embarrassed.

These subjects are ambitious, but they have the patience to wait for things to work out. They love things that give them status but they avoid the flashier symbols of success. Capricorns are interested in business and money and they often do well. Such subjects may be shy when young but they gain confidence and become more sociable as they get older. They can be too easily offended when no offence is intended.

Capricorns make good marriage partners because they truly prefer to be settled in a happy family than flitting from one partner to another. They make good parents because they care about their children and rarely let them down. They particularly adore their parents and they love having them around. These subjects are not as dull as they sound because they can be gently humorous and they can be quite flirtatious. They are often nice looking and they keep their looks when they get old. Capricorns can be insecure and they do best in life if they have an encouraging partner. Most prefer an outgoing partner, and they will do all they can to help that person to get on. Most have a difficult family member somewhere in their lives, but they do what they can for them.

The Sun in Aquarius

Aquarius is a masculine, fixed, air sign that is ruled by Uranus, and in old types of astrology, also by Saturn.

NB: Many people mistake Aquarius for a water sign, because its symbol is the Water Carrier.

Aquarians are clever, friendly, kind, independent and humane. They take a reasonable, unsentimental and impersonal attitude to most things, but they can get very worked up when things go wrong in their own lives. Friendship is often easier for these people than family life, and some of them prefer animals to people. Some Aquarians seem to live in a dream world, finding it hard to get anything done or tackling too many things at one time. These people are so individual that they are unlike anybody else, including other Aquarians! They march to their own drumbeat and live in their own chosen manner. Some of them seem to live entirely inside their own heads, while others throw themselves into causes of one kind or another. Aquarians make excellent teachers and they have a great deal of patience with anyone who is willing to learn. They can express themselves clearly and put points across to others in an imaginative manner. These apparently cool, calm people are actually quite tense inside and sometimes bad tempered. Most can argue the hind leg of a donkey, which is possibly why so many of them love politics. The age of gadgets and technology is made for them, as they seem to have a real affinity for these things.

Aquarian minds are logical and broad-minded, and most of them are clever. Many Aquarians work in the caring professions and they can be excellent counsellors and arbitrators. These subjects make the most loyal and wonderful friends.

The Sun in Pisces

Pisces is a feminine, mutable, water sign, ruled by Neptune, and in old types of astrology, also by Jupiter.

The Sun's energies often turn to such things as teaching, caring for others or developing the spiritual side of life when in Pisces. The creative energies of the Sun are used in a gentle manner and everything is done on a slow and gentle manner. Pisceans are kind hearted.

Pisceans are very hard to quantify because they can present themselves in so many guises. Most of them are gentle and quiet, while some can be surprisingly fiery. Pisceans will rush to give practical help when it is needed. Many of these subjects work in the psychic field because they're drawn to the hidden and mystical sides of life and most are pretty psychic. Despite their gentle, artistic, mystical nature, they are ambitious and often achieve success one way or another. They never seem to earn big money but they always have enough for their needs, and sometimes more than one would suppose. Their biggest fault is a tendency to expect others to run around after them, and some can be surprisingly bossy to their children.

These subjects are often very good with their hands and many of them are gifted artists or musicians. They can create a home out of nothing. Many Pisceans lack confidence and they are very vulnerable when young, but they gain strength in their decision-making abilities later. They do well if matched to a practical and supportive partner and they blossom in a happy family. Some seem to miss the boat where emotional happiness is concerned.

Pisceans can be happy living in a rambling house filled with relatives, children and animals but they also need their own space and time for themselves. Many of these subjects travel to escape, while others bury themselves in a hobby or escape into drink or drugs. Some have a strong hold on life while others seem to have a very tenuous one. Few Pisceans fear death, because they know there is an afterlife.

Chapter Eight: The Moon through the Signs

The Moon in Aries

These subjects are quick thinkers and talkers who are clever large-scale planners but they need help with details. They are starters rather than runners, and they may be happier in an executive position than as one of the workers. Moon in Aries people can be successful in executive positions, but their confidence evaporates quickly and they need the support and admiration of others. Women with this placement need a career. Enthusiastic, headstrong and freedom loving, they cannot take restriction or unnecessary discipline. Such people may have stormy love lives, either because they are changeable and easily bored or because they are unwilling to compromise, but they are usually honest and they don't try to manipulate others.

Moon Aries subjects can be deft and dexterous and their excellent co-ordination can make them successful at sports. The Moon is a water planet and when it is in a fire sign, emotions are expressed quickly and easily. These individuals have hot tempers but they usually cool down again fairly quickly and they rarely sulk for long. They feel entitled to their emotions and are not shy about exhibiting them. In a way, I guess, what you see is what you get! Some are brought up in a military atmosphere or in a family that values sports. Many teach or work in large organisations that benefit the public in some way.

While the childhood is often reasonable, there may be arguments between the individual and the father and this seems to affect father/daughter relationships especially badly. Many grow up to become caring but pushy parents who want the best for their own children.

The Moon in Taurus

This Moon sign is very stable and sensible when the lives of the natives are in perfect working order but when emotional problems come along, these people fall apart. Moon Taurus subjects are pleasant and sociable, respectable, reliable and decent. These subjects need a settled and happy family life, a comfortable home and a good job. They make good parents and successful family members as long as they have the love and support that they need. They are affectionate and romantic and they enter relationships with the best of intentions. They are tough but fair in business and rarely stupid with money. Moon in Taurus people love music, gardening, cooking, the outdoors and travelling. Lunar Taureans seem to love their fathers but they may feel let down by them. The father may be week, ailing or unable to stand up to their mothers. Some experience a childhood that is materially comfortable but lacking in wholehearted love.

The Moon in Gemini

These subjects have active minds that may be academic, imaginative, creative or logical, depending upon other features on the birthchart. They are dexterous and versatile and they can cope with most tasks at work or in the home. Some need freedom and may avoid getting into permanent relationships while others need a practical partner. Some love films and television, while others are into sports. Many work in jobs where they communicate with the public or provide services for the public, such as travel advice, journalism or teaching. Moon in Gemini types stay young, even when they get older.

This Moon placement can indicate a difficult childhood and there may have been problems at school where they suffered from bullying or unfair treatment. They are bright though, and they often love to read when they are young so they tend to educate themselves. They have shrewd minds and excellent business ability, so they do well later in life. They are excellent parents and they keep a close relationship with their children throughout life.

The Moon in Cancer

The Moon rules Cancer, so it is comfortable in this sign. The subjects are sensitive and sometimes moody, imaginative, creative and possibly artistic. They use their intuition in daily life and they may be into religion or psychic subjects. They can be emotionally demanding and moody.

These subjects make good family members and excellent parents, and both sexes are domesticated and many are excellent do-it-yourselves. Lunar Cancerians are shrewd in business matters and sometimes very successful. They don't like taking chances and they need financial and emotional security. They are wonderful teachers and may seek work in that arena. They plan for their old age and they often remain quite youthful in spirit even when old. They love the sea and enjoy travelling with their families. Moon in Cancer subjects normally have quite reasonable parents and they are good to their children.

The Moon in Leo

These people are friendly and welcoming, and while some are genuinely confident, many are quite shy. They are loyal, loving and idealistic and they only leave a partner if it becomes absolutely necessary. They are happiest when they are loved and appreciated. They can put a partner on a pedestal or expect too much from them. These individuals are good organisers who enjoy an orderly life, shouldering responsibility well and having good leadership qualities.

The Lunar Leo childhood is usually good although there may be an emphasis on religion, tradition or educational attainment. The mother is normally warm-hearted and energetic and the childhood home is comfortable and well organised. This is not normally a difficult Moon placement.

The Moon in Virgo

These subjects are keenly intellectual, discriminating and capable of dealing with details. They are emotionally contained, reserved and slow to push themselves forward. They can keep their emotions on a tight leash, being easily embarrassed by displays of emotion. Strong emotions such as anger, jealousy, desire, love and hate may all be buried, denied or deflected into other activities, such as money-making, cleaning the home and so on. This may eventually turn inwards to make them ill.

Moon Virgo folk are keen on matters related to health, hygiene, fitness and alternative therapies. They may be fussy eaters and they are often sensitive to certain types of foods, although many are excellent cooks. Some Lunar Virgoans are timid and full of worries, nerves and negativity, but most are actually rather stubborn and determined. Some can be critical and tactless. These subjects are conscientious providers and excellent at the practical sides of family life, but they may find it hard to show loving feelings to their partners or their children. They make sacrifices for their families. Lunar Virgo subjects are clever with money and they often make shrewd investments and purchases. They work in areas where they can use their communications skills while also helping humanity.

Moon in Virgo subjects have difficult childhoods, and this is probably behind their self-protective attitude. Fortunately, these subjects are not fools and if they take the trouble to look into the reasons behind their unhappiness, they develop the kind of understanding which allows them to change and to grow.

The Moon in Libra

These subjects are charming, optimistic and sociable. They are skilled and tactful diplomats who are popular in all kinds of social settings and some are good looking. Lunar Librans can appear soft, but they are hard workers who can display considerable determination when they have a particular goal in sight. They like having things their way. These subjects don't enjoy being alone, so they seek partnerships in business and personal life and they have many friends. In days gone by, these subjects married young, but nowadays they may live with someone to start with and move on again later but they are faithful when in a stable relationship.

Moon Libra subjects need pleasant living and working surroundings, and they are fussy about decor and colour schemes. They make excellent architects, interior designers and even software designers. Their diplomatic skills can take them into agency work, marketing or union negotiating, and while good company much of the time, they can be arrogant, outspoken and hurtful.

A Moon-Libra childhood is usually a pleasant one with kindly, clever parents who do all they can to stimulate the child's intellect. In some cases, the father is a distant figure, possibly due to business commitments or not being fully committed to family life. There is little strict discipline and everything is reasonable, including the child himself most of the time. These children come under pressure at school, because they can be lazy.

The Moon in Scorpio

Whenever the Moon is in a water sign, the emotions are intense and in Scorpio, the feelings can be quite close to the surface. If these folk are let down in love, they can go on about the situation too much, but if they keep their troubles to themselves, they can fester inside and become ill as a result. Lunar Scorpios never forget those who hurt them but they also remember those who are good to them. These subjects hate to owe money and they hate people who borrow without paying them back. These individuals do best when allied to a cheerful, capable and emotionally stable partner, but their own vulnerability can lead them to choose vulnerable, sensitive or chaotic mates. Although stubborn and inclined to stick to their choices, they can be driven to leave a relationship, but they then learn from their mistakes and go on to make better choices in future.

Lunar Scorpios struggle to achieve financial security but if they suffer financial setbacks, they pick themselves up and to start again. They may experience great gains and losses, and can suffer extremes of tragedy or joy in their lives. They love challenges and they can put a lot into their careers, partnerships and children. They find it easy attract friends, lovers or even money when they put their minds to it. Tough, masculine jobs appeal to some of them while the world of health and healing appeals to others, and they are especially gifted at subjects like psychology and hypnotherapy.

Something seems to have been wrong in the childhood. A parent or sibling may have died; there may have been intense poverty sickness or abandonment. The subject may have become resentful because his brother or sister was more successful and more popular with the parents and grandparents than the Lunar Scorpio was.

The Moon in Sagittarius

There are many Lunar Sagittarians in the worlds of astrology and the psychic sciences and many are excellent dowsers, palmists and anything else of the kind. It seems that these people are driven to explore the inner world of mind, body and spirit and to seek enlightenment at a deep and inner level. Superficially, Lunar Sagittarians are optimistic, outgoing and friendly. Many of them travel a great deal or have strong connections to people from lands, cultures or backgrounds. They seek to learn from these people.

Most Lunar Sagittarians feel the need to contact as many people as they can during their lifetime, which leads them to choose jobs in teaching or dealing with the public. These subjects need personal freedom, so they don't settle with one partner for life, but they keep friendships going for years. Some Lunar Sagittarians relate better to animals than to people. These individuals seem to have pleasant but distant relationships with their parents. They need an interesting lifestyle that offers them plenty of variety. Many are deep thinkers who read, study and expand their knowledge base throughout their lives. These subjects are surprisingly ambitious and they can be quite competitive, which may lead some of them into a sporting lifestyle.

These subjects may have strange childhood experiences in which they are made to feel different from those who are around them. They rarely receive enough nurturing and they miss out on cuddles and affection. They may not stick to one partner for life but they have the ability to draw others to them so they are rarely lonely for long. Lunar Sagittarians can do well at school but they do most of their studying and learning later.

The Moon in Capricorn

These subjects learn early in life that security is hard to find, as they may come from circumstances that are difficult in some way. If the subject himself does not experience severe difficulties in childhood, it is likely that his mother would have suffered, so there is a kind of collective unconsciousness that drives the person to seek financial security. These people work hard and provide for themselves and their families, but they can be too materialistic, too inclined to worry about money and very tight fisted.

It can take a long time before they gain courage and confidence in themselves to open up to others. They may find an outlet in a career or a happy family life later and they overcome most of their problems by patient stoicism. Lunar Capricorns rarely abandon their families or friends. They have a good sense of humour and they are able to laugh at themselves, but they can be touchy and they don't care to have others laugh at them. They have love lives, and they make up in old age for the unhappiness or insecurity of their childhood.

Moon in Aquarius

Lunar Aquarians need independence, and they cannot live under someone else's thumb or be dictated to by others. If any of these subjects have to face a particularly difficult situation, they prefer to do it on their own and without an audience. These subjects are very imaginative and they can be extremely creative. Under stress, these subjects can become aloof, sarcastic or unpredictable. These people are broadminded, always up-to-date and they are keen to live their lives to the full. They can be obstinate, argumentative and keen to have their own way. They need a partner whom they can respect.

These people are very friendly and they keep their friends for a very long time. They are humorous, good company and kind hearted but they can attract too many lame ducks. Many have a strangely distant relationship with their parents, while others are forced to take on the job of parenting their own parents at some point in time. They would have grown up in a household that is full of books and with ample opportunity to obtain a good education, but they tend to prefer having a good time with their friends to putting themselves out at school.

The Moon in Pisces

This Lunar placement can lead the subject into an unusual lifestyle. Many are deeply into mind, body and spirit subjects, and they can be drawn to religion or spiritualism. This Moon placement leads to a great deal of vulnerability and shyness. There is often something wrong in childhood and these natives may feel extremely lonely during childhood and even throughout life. These subjects may choose to be alone for much of the time because the continual presence of other people can upset the delicate balance of their aura. These natives are psychic sponges, who pick up the moods and vibrations of all with whom they come into contact. In some cases, low self-esteem leads to apathy and an inability to get anything done, but when these indecisive worriers have the support of a strong, steadfast and reliable partner they blossom.

These people love deeply and can become obsessed with their lovers. They may not know how to turn down a request, and thus they can allow others to take advantage of their good natures. Sympathetic, romantic and sweet natured, they have an inner strength that comes to the fore in times of crisis, and they have a truly magical gift for helping those who are troubled. Retiring and often in poor health, these strange people achieve more, show more courage and cope with far more than all the other Moon signs of the zodiac put together. Their considerable creative and artistic talents, allied to their instinct for finding gaps in the market means that they find ways of supplying the public with the goods and services that they need. Lunar Pisceans end up surprising others by unexpectedly gaining fame and fortune, and that makes them targets for jealousy.

Chapter Nine: The Personal Planets

Mercury in Aries

The mind is impulsive, quick-witted and the tongue can be sharp and sarcastic. There is often a good memory, particularly for poetry, literary quotations or quiz trivia. The nature is self-assertive and there is a fighting spirit. These subjects can be nervous, impulsive and hyperactive. They may act first and then think later. They concentrate on things that interest them, but skip lightly over other things without studying them deeply.

Mercury in Taurus

The mind is retentive and the thought processes slow but logical. Learning may be easier through pictures than words. This subject is dexterous and practical and may be better with his hands than with academic subjects. Sensible and cheerful, but possibly a bit slow and stodgy, this person can be stubborn, inflexible and incapable of lateral thinking. If nearby planets are in Gemini, this placement acts as a settling or grounding factor.

Mercury in Gemini

These subjects are clever, versatile and inventive, with quick minds. They can think on their feet but they may find it hard to concentrate on one thing at a time. They are excellent communicators who are quick to learn and they can be dexterous or good with computers. They prefer jobs with plenty of variety or opportunities to move from place to place. Highly-strung and nervous, they may talk too much when under stress.

Mercury in Cancer

These people may live in the past or they may take an interest in history or in objects that have historical connections, such as antiques. Their memory is excellent but they are opinionated. They can harbour grudges. Kind and loyal, they dislike major change but they do enjoy novelty and a change of scene from time to time. They may be hypochondriacs.

Mercury in Leo

Optimistic and creative, these subjects can be arrogant, sharp tongued and unfeeling at times. Good public speakers or teachers, they are strong minded and tough in business. They are excellent organisers but they are inclined to get involved in over-optimistic schemes, or carried away with glamorous but unrealistic projects. On the whole, however, these subjects are fairly sensible and they are also generous.

Mercury in Virgo

These subjects are analytical, shrewd and practical, being good at specialisation and problem solving. These individuals may be excellent writers or journalists but they may also be long-winded talkers because they see every detail so clearly and expect others to be as interested in details as they are. These natives are critical of others but even more critical of themselves. Their standards are very high. They have an affinity to the suffering of others and may be interested in healthy living, possibly to the point of hypochondria.

Mercury in Libra

These people are gentle and tactful, and they make excellent ambassadors. They have excellent taste in decor with a strong sense of colour, and they love their creature comforts. They have good business sense but they may lose opportunities through idleness. Sociable and humorous, they can be great fun.

Mercury in Scorpio

The mind is sharp and critical and there may be tendencies towards manipulation, suspicion, jealousy or possessiveness. These subjects may be interested in medical matters, the police or military subjects, and they can be excellent historians or specialists. They can be clever in business but they can lose interest or forget to tie up loose ends. Some are into art or music.

Mercury in Sagittarius

Some of these subjects do well at college while others fall aside when young, but educate themselves later. Broad-minded and lacking in prejudice, these people are interested in everything and everyone. They find it hard to concentrate and they may be involved in so many things that they never really grasp or finish any of them. Frank, versatile and restless, they love travel, foreigners and anything unusual. Some of these subjects are sportsmen and women, while others are drawn to religious or philosophical lifestyles due to their attraction to mystical or spiritual matters.

Mercury in Capricorn

Rational, practical, careful and patient, these subjects take life seriously. Their minds are scientific, mathematical, or attuned to business. Some are keen linguists while others make excellent teachers while others do well in banking or economics. These subjects are traditional in outlook, reliable in business, kind hearted and loyal friends. They do their duty!

Mercury in Aquarius

Intuitive, inventive, modern and interested in science and social progress, these subjects are excellent communicators who may choose to work for the public. A detached attitude makes them appear to be good judges of human behaviour, but they may be too distanced to really understand others. They can have an unrealistic outlook.

Mercury in Pisces

Intuitive, imaginative, flexible and kind, these people have broad minds and they are drawn to mysticism, spirituality and the meaning of life and the after life. Many are clairvoyant and spiritual, while others are very creative and imaginative. They can be chaotic and prone to escapism through drink, drugs or sex. Over emotional, secretive and manipulative, these subjects lack confidence, but they find ways of succeeding anyway. These people can be drawn to spiritual healing.

~~~~~~~~~~

Venus in Aries

Affectionate and sexy, these people are fond of giving unusual presents. They enjoy social life and outings. They are creative, popular and flirtatious. They can be headstrong and reckless with money or fluctuate between generosity and meanness. They aren't bothered about possessions, although they will value their sports equipment, motorcar and they may collect unusual items.

Venus in Taurus

These people are affectionate and passionate. Some are into cooking, eating, art, music or crafts. They can be self-indulgent but they are shrewd with money, being careful and possibly somewhat tight fisted. They need a nice home and a great garden.

Venus in Gemini

Flirtatious, light-hearted, restless and possibly fickle, some of these subjects feel trapped by close personal relationships. They are fond of their relatives. Some love travel, music, art and drama. Although adaptable, some find themselves the odd one out in their family. They love to collect books or equipment although they are actually more interested in ideas than in goods.

Venus in Cancer

Affectionate and sympathetic, these people may smother their loved ones or lean on them. Emotional, clinging and imaginative, these subjects react badly to loss or rejection. They are home loving, good cooks and good hosts. They love history and antiques and need a nice home and garden. They may spend their lives seeking security. They need a settled relationship and money in the bank. They may be subject to weight gain.

Venus in Leo

These subjects need love but they may dominate their partners. They are generous and loving, and they love their children deeply. They love good clothes and a nice home. They can be creative and they love to produce goods that others admire. They are flirtatious and fun. They usually obtain property and goods during their lives.

Venus in Virgo

These people can be critical of others but they are even more self-critical, which leads to low self-esteem. They hate dirt and mess. They can be sexy, but while they seek close and loving relationships, they may not find them until later in life. Although reserved and quietly charming, they may be fault finding or fussy. They have good practical business sense and can be shrewd but while they like money, they aren't hoarders and they can spend freely.

Venus in Libra

Kind hearted, lovable and sociable, these people are nice looking with really lovely eyes. They find it hard to maintain one strong relationship if it requires effort, and they may drift away from lovers and friends. They are very artistic and probably also musical. Despite their gentle, dreamy nature, they are good in business and not as soft as they look.

Venus in Scorpio

Sensual, passionate and possessive, these subjects hang onto what is theirs, and they don't forgive a hurt. They can be extremely generous or amazingly stingy. They often have executive ability but their pig-headed attitude can spoil their efforts. Some of them are jealous of the ability of others. They are not especially acquisitive, being more interested in a good lifestyle than in accumulating things. These subjects make good and loyal friends but they can take advantage of those who they perceive as being weak. This placement also indicates strong intuition, with possible clairvoyant powers and a need to be close to the spiritual side of life.

Venus in Sagittarius

These subjects must feel free. They choose jobs where they can come and go as they please and they love to travel. Some are very adventurous and unsettled, so they may delay marriage until late in life. Some are spiritual and psychic. Most are humanitarian and idealistic but they can be tactless and thoughtless. They only need money for the freedom it allows them, as they aren't particularly into possessions. They make good friends and very good teachers.

Venus in Capricorn

Conventional and stable in matters of affection, these people can be undemonstrative, but they can actually be quite sexy. They may be calculating and fussy at work and also status conscious. They are reliable workers who will get on with things if left in peace. If challenged, they dig their heels in and fight back hard. They are shrewd and business like. They are deeply into their family and very caring towards older family members. They value education, art and literature, but also money making.

Venus in Aquarius

These subjects don't like conventional jobs or home life, and they need to feel that they can come and go as they please. They can cope with a lot because they don't become too attached to anyone or anything. They are friendly and helpful to others but they don't like people who cling to them. Possessions aren't as important to them as being with people who share their ideas and their needs.

Venus in Pisces

These subjects are creative, artistic or musical and they may be very good looking. They are emotional and sentimental. They need a creative outlet or one that allows them to express themselves. They may sacrifice too much for loved ones or their families. Some are sensible with money while others aren't, while some are generous and others tight fisted. They are often misunderstood.

~~~~~~~~~~

Mars in Aries

Argumentative, outspoken, impulsive and obstinate, such subjects can be a real handful. They may appear self-assured on the surface but they may actually be quite unsure of themselves underneath. There is a small child hidden not too far under the surface and it is this that makes them so attractive. Other attractive features are their openness and friendliness, in addition to their intelligence and their witty sense of humour. They may be practical with mechanical talent and they may love gadgets. They may be prone to fevers, high blood pressure, eye troubles and accidents to the head.

Mars in Taurus

These people are hard practical workers who have the strength of character and obstinacy to finish what they start. Some of these subjects are good singers or dancers, and many are clever cooks, gardeners or craft workers.

These people have a smouldering and somewhat grudging temperament, and they don't like to be opposed or deflected from their chosen path. Passionate about life and love, they have strong feelings that are not always apparent to others, while they can be secretive and quite difficult to live with. These subjects have excellent organising talents and shrewd business abilities. They like money and they can be sexy.

Clever, talented and dexterous, these subjects may not have the staying power to finish what they start. Talkative, restless and nervous, they need a life that does not give them too many problems. These subjects are clever inventors and problem-solvers but they are easily bored by too much routine or detail. They are adaptable and interested in travel and communications. There may be a tendency to accidents to the hands, shoulders and arms.

Mars in Cancer

Ambitious and clinging, emotional, sensitive and sensuous, these subjects need security and they need to be loved and cared for. Both sexes are domesticated and may be good at cooking, do-it-yourself jobs and creative gardening. These people make excellent but rather possessive parents and marriage partners and they may also be inclined to lean on their spouses. Very intuitive and probably psychic, these subjects may be attracted to the psychic sciences. They may have weak stomachs or (if female) sensitive breasts.

Mars in Leo

These folk like excitement and change and cannot put up with a dull or routine job. They enjoy travel, meeting new people and tackling a variety of problems. They appear confident but this may be something of a pose. They are attractive and popular and they have friendly personalities. There may be problems with the spine or the heart.

Mars in Virgo

These subjects should be hard workers but sometimes they spend more time talking and fiddling about than actually doing anything, but when their interest is aroused, they can get on extremely well and at great speed. These people need a job that holds their attention and which provides them with plenty of variety because boredom is their worst enemy. They are quite shrewd operators and they are capable of attending to details. They are drawn to work in the communications or medical industries. These people can be too critical and nervous fussy and demanding and they may talk too much. Worry makes them ill and their weak spots are the bowels and skin.

Mars in Libra

These subjects are clever and perceptive about people. They are interested in communicating with others and they may be good business people. These people are friendly and sociable but they can be very laid back and rather lazy. They have a strong survival instinct and they will fight hard for what is theirs. Mars in Libra people are flirtatious and very fond of the opposite sex. Their marriage-type relationships should have a strongly sexual content. Their weak spots are the kidneys, pancreas and bladder.

Mars in Scorpio

These subjects have very strong characters and they can bully weaker types. They aim high and work hard for their chosen goals. They can be secretive, relentless and even cruel at times. They are very perceptive, intuitive and even quite psychic. They may be interested in the occult or anything that is hidden. Some choose to work as detectives while others are drawn to the military life. They need self-discipline and an organised lifestyle. As far as health is concerned, they are very strong and resilient, but they can drink too much and they may suffer spinal or reproductive problems.

Mars in Sagittarius

Boisterous and energetic, these people may take life by storm. They are independent thinkers who may choose unusual or unconventional lifestyles. Some are sceptical and questioning, while others are drawn to mysticism and astrology. They love travel, sports and adventure. Some are outspoken, tactless and argumentative, while others use their intellect to fight injustice wherever they see it. Some never really settle down but drift from one partner to another throughout their lives. Some are very sexually experimental. Their weak spots are the hips, thighs and arteries.

Mars in Capricorn

These people are strong characters and they may be power hungry and obstinate. They have excellent organisational ability and they can be practical, self-reliant and capable. They can also be cold, distant and irritable, but they do get things done. They hate waste. Their health areas are the ears, teeth, bones, knees and skin.

Mars in Aquarius

These individuals are impulsive and idealistic, so they are often found working for good causes. They may be intellectual but also unpredictable, while they can also be determined and obstinate. They may find it hard to express their feelings. They need freedom and they don't like to be smothered or for anyone to get in their way. Their health problem areas are their circulation, ankles and legs.

Mars in Pisces

Some of these people are self-sacrificial, emotional and lacking in drive and concentration, while others are artistic and dreamy. Some make exceptional designers and engineers who do very well when allowed to work on their own projects. They can be unrealistic. They love music, dance and the arts. They can be penny wise and pound-foolish. Some are psychic and spiritual. The weak spots are the feet, lungs and circulation.

Chapter Ten: The Transpersonal Planets

Jupiter takes about a year to traverse a sign, while Saturn takes about two and a half years to do so.

Jupiter in Aries

Self-sufficient, freedom loving, honest and extravagant, these subjects can be overly optimistic, reckless or thoughtless. They may bully others. They need to learn to budget their time, money and energy. They can be clever workers who do well in large organisations. They value freedom to express their opinions but they also value the organisations to which they belong.

Jupiter in Taurus

These people love comfort, rich living and good food, and they may overindulge in all of these things. They have sound judgement and their feet are on the ground. They are, for the most part, good-hearted, reliable friends and steady workers. They can be possessive or materialistic. They enjoy practical work, especially if it is on a large scale, such as construction work or landscape gardening. These people value what they can see, hear, feel, taste and touch.

Jupiter in Gemini

These people are clever but possibly somewhat superficial. They make good teachers and journalists and they can be affable but unreliable as friends. Mentally alert, versatile and good conversationalists, they need constant stimulation because they are easily bored. They enjoy word games and literature and they are dexterous and inventive, valuing ideas and intellectual freedom. They love to travel and explore. They can be crafty.

Jupiter in Cancer

These individuals are kind, good-humoured and sympathetic. They are more ambitious than one realises and they can be restless. They are emotional by nature and they can become emotionally attached to job, a house, an area or an idea. They are sociable, patriotic and fairly old-fashioned in their values. Such people are loyal to their families but their possessiveness and touchiness can make them hard to live with. They may draw invisible lines which one crosses at one's peril. These subjects have good business sense but they can incline towards nepotism especially where their parents are concerned. They can make money from antiques.

Jupiter in Leo

The natives are big-hearted, generous and creative. They can be popular and they have the ability to draw people and for the public to like them. They are intelligent, honest and vital, and they like to live in a glamorous or exciting world. They can be overbearing, pompous and arrogant. They enjoy prestige and money and like to do everything on a grand scale. Their work brings them fame but not always fortune. They love to teach or train others. These humorous people enjoy music and dancing and they feel that life is for living.

Jupiter in Virgo

These people are kind, conscientious, moral and ethical. They have an analytical approach to their work. They should try not to bottle up their emotions or divert too many of their feelings into their work. They enjoy research, analysis and intellectual pursuits and they may have success in the medical or scientific fields. They can be critical, pernickety or absent-minded. These people value material goods, money, education and ideas.

Jupiter in Libra

These subjects are sympathetic, kind, harmonious and charitable. They work best in a partnership or as part of a team, although they can be lazy and self-indulgent. They are interested in legal matters and may work in that field. They enjoy music, art, literature and culture. They need to be admired or praised and they value marriage and companionship.

Jupiter in Scorpio

These folk are often sexy, and they live life to the full. They can be dramatic and self-centred. These subjects are shrewd, ambitious and strong-willed. They can overwork or overdo almost anything to which they set their minds. These individuals may be proud and conceited but they can also relate to the underdog or to the animal world. They love a challenge and they enjoy seeking out things that are hidden, solving mysteries and solving problems.

Some subjects are very drawn to the occult. They value personal achievement and strength of character.

Jupiter in Sagittarius

These subjects are optimistic, forward thinking and philanthropic. They may choose to work the law, the church or the travel trade. They are supposed to like large animals but they seem to actually prefer small ones. These people are sympathetic and kind, but they may be erratic and tactless. They are broad-minded and they enjoy travelling or being in the company of foreigners. Most of them enjoy visiting wide-open spaces. They may be a bit lazy and inclined to let things drift or they may jump from one idea to the next without getting anything done. Many of these subjects are intuitive and interested in astrology or the psychic and mystical world. They value personal freedom, independence and intelligence.

Jupiter in Capricorn

These subjects are resourceful, responsible and thoughtful. They can be stingy, penny-wise and pound-foolish, austere and cold. On the other hand, they can be productive and thorough. They work hard and may put their jobs before personal relationships. Some of these subjects can be egotistical, unsociable and unpopular, but they are deep thinkers, and they value structure and old-fashioned ideas. They may value the Earth and all that is in it, and they may seek to save it in practical ways.

Jupiter in Aquarius

Humanitarian, impartial and imaginative, these subjects can be tactless, unpredictable, restless or obstinate and wilful. They are high-minded, idealistic and attached to causes, but they may be unrealistic. These subjects need a definite goal to focus upon. They can be extremely intuitive and very attracted to astrology or the occult. They work hard on group projects, and they value freedom, intellect and working for the betterment of the world.

Jupiter in Pisces.

This is a good placement for work in the medical or the caring professions. These subjects are intuitive, imaginative and artistic. They are kind, humane, romantic and idealistic, but they can become detached from reality. These people need clear goals, and they can be psychic, spiritual and attracted to the occult.

~~~~~~~~~~

Saturn in Aries

This results in a seesaw personality that can be nice or nasty depending upon mood. These people are ambitious, determined and self-reliant, or jealous, defiant and impatient. They may have a good eye for mechanical matters or they may be into computing. They could be interested in military matters. They may have had a destructive parent or possibly a rough time at school, and they may have difficulty in expressing themselves or in being themselves. They can achieve high esteem.

Saturn in Taurus

Patient, cautious, methodical and economical, these subjects can be frugal and obstinate but they know how to persevere and they may produce things of beauty. They work well under pressure but hate to be rushed. There may be a background of poverty and of life in uncongenial places, or over-materialistic parents.

Saturn in Gemini

Logical, conscientious and serious, these subjects can be deeply intellectual, very dexterous and they have the patience to complete long and complex tasks. They may be good at maths, astrology and science and they make thorough and well-prepared teachers. Their early education is poor and they may suffer from bullying at school, but they make up for it later. The father may have left home, disappeared or died. The person would have been lonely as a child. He lived in the world of books and imagination.

Saturn in Cancer

Shrewd, ambitious, tenacious and hard working, these subjects are very attached to their families and they may try to control them. These people are emotionally controlled and they can become melancholy or self-absorbed. One of the parents or parent figures could have made the childhood home unhappy.

Saturn in Leo

This subject could be self-assured or very self-effacing, depending upon how Saturn affects them. There is excellent organising ability and a natural attitude of authority. They may have a good deal of knowledge about something glamorous, such as jewellery or fashion. Some find it hard to relax and enjoy life. Some have bad-tempered or disciplinarian parents or ungrateful children.

Saturn in Virgo

These subjects are methodical, prudent and tidy but they can critical, faultfinding and mistrustful. They have high personal standards and they are good at keeping confidences. They are good at detailed or analytical work and may be drawn to editing or the medical world. They tend to mistrust the motives of others. They may have had cold or demanding parents.

Saturn in Libra

On one hand, these individuals may be lonely due to failed partnerships, even though they are kind, pleasant and honourable. They can work hard for a chosen goal or in order to right an injustice and they can be successful, probably due to Saturn being exalted in Libra. Their parents are reasonable people, but there is a possibility that one of the parents was weak or that one deserted the family.

Saturn in Scorpio

These people are resilient and capable. They have executive ability and a shrewd idea of what will or won't work and can be very successful in business. They can hold a grudge and punish others, be ruthless, jealous, possessive and inflexible. They can also be impractical. However, they love deeply and can be very good to their loved ones.

Saturn in Sagittarius

This softens Saturn's tendency to dourness, so it's a good placement, but it can make the person hurtful and tactless or dedicated to strange causes. These subjects are forward-looking and keen on higher education for themselves and others. They can be religious, philosophical and intellectual but they can also be fanatical.

Saturn in Capricorn

Methodical, hard working, disciplined and ambitious, these subjects advance slowly in life and overcome obstacles. They can be selfish, pessimistic and they may worry unnecessarily over money but they are generally sensible and often successful in business or politics. They can have a dry sense of humour. They are attached to their parents and other family members.

Saturn in Aquarius

These folk are serious, intellectual and good thinkers. They may have scientific or mathematical abilities. If they decide to work for causes, they do so in a thorough manner and they finish what they start. These people are reserved but quite sociable, especially towards their families and their trusted friends. They also have a dry and witty sense of humour. They are forgiving and balance but also judgemental and somewhat opinionated. They can lead lonely lives.

Saturn in Pisces

This is an excellent placement for those who work in the medical profession, teaching or the church. These subjects are humanitarian, idealistic and romantic, and they implement their beliefs in a realistic manner. They can be indecisive, mood and manipulative, and their strong emotional nature can bring them problems. They need a steady partner and a secure home life.

Chapter Eleven: The Impersonal Planets

These planets exert a generational influence, due to their slow and distant orbits, although Chiron only takes around two years to traverse a sign.

Uranus in Aries

These people are freedom loving, unconventional, positive and independent. They could be inventive engineers or craft workers. There may be unexpected events in life and the grandparents could be a strong influence.

Uranus in Taurus

These subjects have fixed opinions, and are headstrong, resourceful, disruptive and intense. They attack problems forcefully. They have sudden financial ups and downs and also strange values. They may inherit money from grandparents.

Uranus in Gemini

Versatile, imaginative and nervy, these people may have telepathic ability. They have unusual brothers and sisters or an unusual family situation, as well as an unusual education and possibly an unusual career. Grandparents could have a hand in the subject's education or upbringing.

Uranus in Cancer

These subjects may be emotionally unstable, touchy and eccentric. An original or unusual domestic life may be chosen. They may have had a disrupted childhood, possibly brought up by grandparents.

Uranus in Leo

Hard working, adventurous, bold, defiant and powerful, these subjects may have interesting children or be interested in child development. They may be domineering and eccentric. Such subjects may have strange grandparents who were a strong influence in childhood or a powerful father.

Uranus in Virgo

There may be an interest in diet and health, cleanliness and alternative therapies. These subjects have good critical faculties and could be inventive teachers. They may be funny about food and they may have strange but rather distant grandparents.

Uranus in Libra

This signifies a dual personality that is both charming and disruptive. There is definite evidence of an unusual marriage or partnerships. They have literary ability and a fondness for television and the media. They are scientific, artistic, and possibly psychic. They may have loving grandparents.

Uranus in Scorpio

These people could be somewhat odd, swinging between being very helpful to others and then being dictatorial or distant. These subjects can be independent, determined and emotional but they can also be vindictive and explosive. Weird grandparents may have brought them up.

Uranus in Sagittarius

These people may be reckless and independent with some really original ideas about life, love, religion and the world in general. They reach out for higher knowledge or spiritual understanding. They may have grown up with grandparents who emigrated from one country to another, bringing knowledge of a different culture with them.

Uranus in Capricorn

These people may be interested in politics and they may live through a time of change. With penetrating minds and an authoritative manner, they may be rebellious and domineering or thoughtful and thorough. They come from family backgrounds that encourage their ambition.

Uranus in Aquarius

Resourceful and clever, intuitive and imaginative, these subjects may be into astrology or the psychic sciences. They have original ideas for reform and an interest in science. They are modern thinkers who are humanitarian and idealistic but they may be cool and mechanical. They seem to come from clever families.

Uranus in Pisces

This person will look into religion and mysticism. Highly intuitive, secretive and emotional with changeable moods, they may have mediumistic dreams. They are great ups and downs in life, with scandals and losses, balanced by sudden gains in status and wealth.

~~~~~~~~~~

Neptune in Aries

These subjects have unusual personalities. They are emotional, romantic and artistic, and they love to travel. They may be interested in psychic research or some strange form of politics. This links people to the enterprising eras of discovery and development.

Neptune in Taurus

Musical, artistic and creative, they may work in the arts. They experience fluctuating finances. This links to the early stages of modern banking and business practices, also to a better way of life for most people.

Neptune in Gemini

These people are mystical, imaginative and prophetic with many new ideas on religion. They may be peevish and gossipy. This links to the spread of education for ordinary people.

Neptune in Cancer

These individuals are emotional and imaginative. They choose artistic home surroundings and they love the sea. This links to the start of ordinary people having decent housing and enjoying the cinema and theatre.

Neptune in Leo

There is an interest in glamour and escapist entertainment, so they love dance, film and the theatre. They are dramatic, artistic, magnetic and often kind hearted. This links people to the glamour of Hollywood during the Second World War.

Neptune in Virgo

Critical of orthodox religion, they may be intellectual, intuitive and sensitive. They may suffer from allergies to food and drugs. They are interested in nutrition and health matters. This links people to the Welfare State, National Insurance and the National Health Service.

Neptune in Libra

These subjects are gentle, artistic, romantic and keen on love. They also love music and the poetry inherent in much popular music. They dislike war and materialism. This links people to the hippy and New Age era.

Neptune in Scorpio

These people are sensitive, emotional and mediumistic. They may be secretive with a strong sense of justice. They overturn their parents' religious or social beliefs. This links people to improvements in medicine but also new health scares.

Neptune in Sagittarius

These individuals love travel and new ideas. They may look for new religious ideas. There is an interest in research, language and literature. This is when religion begins to grow again, including the revival of Wicca and paganism.

Neptune in Capricorn

This links practical ability with business insight and inspiration. Changes in religious outlook start to connect with ideas, such as power, domination, control and money in some cases and a love the earth and a dislike of materialism in others.

Neptune in Aquarius

Natives with this sign will look for new ideas, philosophies and ways of life. They may be idealistic but unrealistic and they may have new ideas about religion, love, marriage, romance and the social order. This links people with different ideas about marriage, gay marriage and the rise of different religious ideas.

Neptune in Pisces

Mysterious religions are signified here, and this generation might reach the heights or sink into the depths of depravity, possibly making their religion an excuse for their bad behaviour. Allergies and strange ailments will abound.

Chapter Twelve: Dwarf Planets through the Signs

Pluto in Gemini – 1900 to 1914

- A time of scientific discoveries and new means of transport.
- The rise of socialism and trades unions.
- Universal education in Europe and America.
- Beginning of film, which educates and entertains the populace.

Pluto in Cancer – 1914 to 1939

- The horror of the First World War and families broken up by the war.
- Fight for better rights for ordinary people.
- Depression and financial desperation.
- House prices tumble but much good council house building.
- Government impinges more on the lives of ordinary people.

Pluto in Leo – 1939 to 1958

- Wars of ideology, bringing death on a mega scale.
- Famines and disease in other countries.
- Rationing and austerity in the West
- Rise of Welfare State, National Health Service, child welfare.
- The Marshall Plan and post war reconstruction.
- Rise of democracy but also communism.

Pluto in Virgo – 1958 to 1971

- Changes in social and sexual rules.
- Improvements in health, living and working conditions.
- Analytical attitude to world problems.
- Rise of TV news broadcasting and TV age.
- The Vietnam War, civil rights, women's liberation.
- Beginning of space exploration.

Pluto in Libra – 1971 to 1983

- Changes in methods of business.
- New attitudes to marriage and family life.
- Women's lib and racial equality.
- Striving to end war and nuclear threat.
- Real interest in ecology.
- First real power struggles over oil and fuel.

Pluto in Scorpio – 1983 to 1995

- Soviet Union and communism ends.
- Reduction in nuclear arms, but changes in power bases.
- AIDS, but also openness about sexual behaviour.
- Changes in family structure.
- Changes in oil and fuel industry.
- Rise of terrorism.

Pluto in Sagittarius – 1995 to 2008

- Rise of Islam.
- Rise of terrorism.
- Major wars in the Middle East.
- Welfare state at its height, but beginning to tail off.
- New technology changes communications and transport.
- Ordinary people relatively well off.
- Hidden problems in banking and governments.
- Space exploration grows.

Pluto in Capricorn – 2008 to 2024

- Bad banking practices exposed.
- Fiddles and scandals in high places exposed.
- Recession and possibly depression.
- Trying to extract the West from Middle East wars, but with limited success.
- Space exploration still growing.
- Health improves in some ways but bad lifestyles take their toll.

~~~~~~~~~~

Chiron in Aries

- Accidents to the head, eyes and upper jaw.
- Desire to be independent but this is hard to achieve.
- Difficult relationship with the father.

Chiron in Taurus

- Health issues in the throat, lower jaw or neck.
- Health issues affecting the bladder or lower spine.

- Issues in the family regarding money, goods and inheritance.

Chiron in Gemini

- Health issues relating to the hands, arms, shoulders and lungs.
- Family problems with siblings.
- Living in a difficult neighbourhood or with difficult neighbours.
- Educational problems.

Chiron in Cancer

- Problems with lungs, chest area or breasts.
- Difficulties with mother or mother figures.
- Hard to get or keep a nice home.

Chiron in Leo

- Accidents and problems with the spine and heart.
- Desire for success but this is hard to achieve.
- Difficulties with father figures.

Chiron in Virgo

- Digestive and bowel problems.
- Problems with hands, arms or shoulders.
- Problems with siblings and other relatives.

Chiron in Libra

- Problems with kidneys or bladder.
- Problems with lower spine and mobility.

- Too much or too little discipline.
- Marriage, divorce, or partnerships very good or very bad.

Chiron in Scorpio

- Problems with reproductive organs or bowels.
- Head injuries or problems with head and eyes.
- Financial problems, due to banking, legal or inheritance matters.
- Marriage, divorce or partnerships very good or very bad.

Chiron in Sagittarius

- Problems with hips and thighs.
- Problems with siblings.
- Delayed or poor education.
- Problems with travel, religion or the law.

Chiron in Capricorn

- Health issues with knees, bones and ears.
- Problems with skin, lungs and arteries.
- Financial problems not of one's making.
- Responsibilities and problems related to father figures.

Chiron in Aquarius

- Health issues with legs and ankles, also skin.
- Problems with arteries.
- Great ideas but others may not take the person seriously.
- Revolutions and changes disrupt normal life.

Chiron in Pisces

- Health issues affecting the feet, lungs and mental state.
- Religious or political changes may disrupt life.
- Mysteries, swindles, scandals and weird things may happen from time to time.

Chiron Transits

I don't deal with predictive astrology in this book, but as there still isn't much practical information around on the Chiron effect, it's worth mentioning it here. Chiron takes around 51 years to orbit the Sun, but it has an eccentric orbit in the area between Saturn and Uranus. As an early watcher of the Chiron effect, I discovered that most people go through some kind of upheaval when Chiron reaches its "return" at around the age of fifty-one. Any transit of Chiron, from sextile, square, trine, opposition or return, will bring a dose of reality or a change of direction. It often connects with health problems, especially accidents and operations, menopause, the start of a long illness, the break-up of a partnership, falling deeply in love, the start of a new relationship, a change of career, a move of house or a change of country.

~~~~~~~~~~

Asteroids

I sometimes use Ceres and Vesta in readings because they have pleasant effects on a chart, which helps to balance the preponderance of harsh influences. Ceres brings financial benefits in both the natal and transiting chart, while Vesta improves home life.

Chapter Thirteen: Angles, Hemispheres, Elements and Qualities

The Ascendant (Asc)

The ascendant is the degree of the sign of the zodiac that was coming up over the horizon when a new baby made his first cry, or at the start of a new enterprise. You can see the Asc in action by running an Astro-Cartography chart, being sure to include the ecliptic, then run a line from the person's place of birth to the Sun's rise line, and finally, to drop a line downwards from that point to the ecliptic. If none of that makes any sense to you, don't worry about it, just make up your chart in your usual way and use the Asc that your software gives you.

The ascendant relates to the kind of programming the person received in childhood from his family, school, friends and society. Thus, it has a bearing on a subject's outer manner, his appearance and the way he lives. It may determine the kind of career he takes up. The ascendant is linked to the first house and thus to a person's physical health and appearance and personal manner. Nothing is cut and dried in astrology, but the ascendant is a strong modifying factor on a chart and it is often more obvious than the Sun sign. Any planet that is close to the ascendant will have a powerful effect on the subject's personality and lifestyle.

The Descendant (Dsc)

This is the cusp of the seventh house and it is always found opposite the ascendant. We tend to choose people as partners, lovers and colleagues who have the kind of character and values which can be found in the sign on the descendant. Planets close to the descendant can show the influence that others have on us or perhaps the way we think about relationships.

The Midheaven,
Also Known as the Medium Coeli or MC

In all house systems other than equal house, the MC is the cusp of the tenth house, and it can be found at or near the top of the chart. The MC denotes direction a person tries to take in life and it can indicate career choices or what someone tries to achieve. Planets around the Midheaven suggest a need for public recognition, and they can denote a search for something that the father failed to provide. The MC can also show the choice of marriage partner.

The Nadir,
Also Known as the Immum Coeli or IC

In any system other than the equal house system, this is the cusp of the fourth house, and it can be found at or near the bottom of the birthchart. This relates to a person's past, his family background or where he came from. It also speaks about his or her home and domestic circumstances. It concerns the circumstances that prevailed at the beginning of a subject's life and those that might apply at the end of his life. It may throw some light on his relationships with his parents, especially his mother. Planets in this area show a need for financial or emotional security.

Hemispheres

Bear in mind that any astrological chart points to the south! So if you want to make sense of how it works, sit or stand facing the south and look at the position of the sun in the sky.

The upper hemisphere contains the 7th, 8th, 9th, 10th, 11th and 12th houses. A subject with most of his planets in this part of his chart will not be too deeply affected by the actions of other people and he may be able to distance himself from those around him. He keeps his eye on the main chance or on his own needs and feelings, but also on the needs of humanity in general. He needs a career or lifestyle that fulfils him. If the planets are grouped in the 8th, 9th or 12th houses, the subject will have strong spiritual needs and will see life in terms of related spiritual values. If in the 10th, he will be ambitious and politically astute, while if they are in the 11th, he will be interested in humanity in general and education in particular.

The lower hemisphere contains the 1st, 2nd, 3rd, 4th, 5th and 6th houses, and someone who has most of his planets in this part of the chart will be sensitive to the moods and feelings of those around him and he may suffer a good deal as a result. His family may bully him or wear him down, or he may live through his family rather than for himself. He may be too subjective or he may choose to do most of his thinking and working at home.

The eastern hemisphere contains the 10th, 11th, 12th, 1st, 2nd and 3rd houses. A subject who has most of his planets in this area of the chart is a self-starter who chooses his own path through life and sets his own boundaries. He is not happy living off other people or being kept by someone else, and other people don't do much for him. When the planets are in the first three houses, the subject is self-absorbed and convinced that his own opinions are the only ones that matter.

The western hemisphere contains the 4th, 5th, 6th, 7th, 8th and 9th houses. A subject who has most of his planets in this area of the chart will use diplomacy to keep others on his side. Others may look after him or he may spend his life supporting and motivating others. When the majority of planets are in the 6th, 7th and 8th houses, he will use his energy to fulfil the needs of others. This subject may bring up several children.

The Elements

The element of fire:

The key ideas here are of enthusiasm, initiative, intuition, optimism and faith in the future. Fiery people never quite relinquish their childhood, so they are in tune with young people and young ideas. These entertaining people display considerable egotism but also spontaneous generosity. They get things started, create action and pace but they may leave the details to others. Fire sign people are quick to grasp an idea and they approach life with a degree of sportsmanship as if it were a kind of game. These people find it difficult to save money but they can usually earn their way out of disaster. Fire subjects have very hot tempers but once they have shouted and raved a little, the steam goes out of them and they settle back into their usual good-humoured nature, although Leos can hold grudges.

The element of earth:

This element is concerned with security, structure, slow growth, conventional behaviour and concrete results. Earth people are sensible, possibly rather plodding and practical in outlook. They do things thoroughly and carefully and they are unlikely to be extravagant. They are very caring towards family and friends. They hold on to their possessions and may be a little too money-minded at times.

They try to finish any job that they start. There is a sense of maturity with these people but perhaps a lack of spontaneity. Their virtue is their reliability and their vice, fussiness. They are slow to rouse to anger but they can be very angry indeed if hurt.

The element of air:

This element is concerned with networks of all kinds, along with education, theoretical ideas, finding answers to questions and all-round enlightenment. These subjects may be serious-minded or they can be chirpy, streetwise people. They can be found expounding on a pet idea or arguing a point over anything from a literary reference to a sporting event. They make good journalists and shopkeepers, teachers and travellers because they are always up to date. Although kind-hearted, they tend to forget their friends when out of sight. They are not especially hot-tempered but they can become extremely angry over an injustice.

The element of water:

Water people respond slowly when asked a question and they may appear slow when grasping a new concept. However, they are not slow or stupid, it's just that they need time for everything to filter through their highly intuitive aura before it hits the brain. Water people are slow to change, preferring to stay on a tried and tested path. Their chief need is financial security, and this is sometimes hard for them to obtain. Faithful, loyal and rather tense, water people have an intuitive feeling for what is right for themselves and their families. They are usually sensible and reliable but if their feelings are stirred up, they can react strangely. They can become depressed and ill if they are not loved enough. Water people are very sympathetic to the needs of others and they appreciate artistic or creative matters. These people don't lose their temper easily but they can be very destructive to themselves or others when they do, but their biggest problem is that they make decisions based on their feelings rather than on logic.

The Qualities

The cardinal signs:

Cardinal sign people are ambitious for themselves, their families and if appropriate, their organisation. There is a dynastic feel to all these signs and, once they have found the right avenue for their talents, they go as far as they can. They don't listen to others very much as they only really value their own opinions and they like having their own way.

The fixed signs:

Fixed people don't like change. They stick to their jobs, homes and families through thick and thin and they have the strength and determination to see things through. They may stick in a bad job or a bad relationship too long. These subjects are all stubborn and determined and they work hard to obtain financial security and to keep it.

The mutable signs:

Mutable people have the courage to go their own way and do things differently, so many choose an alternative lifestyle, change countries or just life in a way that is different from the rest of their family and friends. They are adaptable and they will fit in with most situations and most types of people. They try a point of contact or understanding between themselves and even the oddest people. Their thinking is wider and more lateral than the other two types and their friendliness and good humour make them good fun to be with. They have jobs or lifestyles that lead many people or things to pass through their hands. They can suffer from loneliness.

Chapter Fourteen: The Houses

There are twelve houses on a birthchart, starting from the ascendant and working their way round the chart in an anti-clockwise direction. There are many house systems to choose from, and each country seems to have its favourites, as do many astrologers. We tend to use those that feel right, and our choices are entirely subjective. I use Placidus for character reading, but I will also check out equal house, especially when it comes to predictive work.

Each house is linked to a sign:

HOUSE	SIGN
First	Aries
Second	Taurus
Third	Gemini
Fourth	Cancer
Fifth	Leo
Sixth	Virgo
Seventh	Libra
Eighth	Scorpio
Ninth	Sagittarius
Tenth	Capricorn
Eleventh	Aquarius
Twelfth	Pisces

Each house is linked to one or more planets:

HOUSE	PLANET
First	Mars
Second	Venus
Third	Mercury
Fourth	Moon
Fifth	Sun
Sixth	Mercury, Chiron
Seventh	Venus
Eighth	Pluto, Mars
Ninth	Jupiter
Tenth	Saturn
Eleventh	Uranus, Saturn
Twelfth	Neptune, Jupiter

A Brief Introduction to the Houses

If the ascendant falls near the beginning of a sign, the sign will occupy most of the first house, but if it falls towards the end of the sign, there will be a small part of the sign in the first house, but the next sign along will take up most of the first house. I am a good example of this, as I am Gemini rising, but my ascendant is 25 deg. Gemini, so only four degrees fall in Gemini and most of my first house is Cancer. The shape and layout of the houses can be further complicated by the house system that you decide to use.

The First House

*Similar to Aries and Mars, and
it is an Angular house.*

Many people resemble their rising sign, and it often represents the person's outward appearance and mode of behaviour, but sometimes the Sun sign or some other factor is stronger. Unfortunately, there are no hard and fast rules and one has to approach each chart with an open mind.

The first house should rule the subject's looks, outer manner and some aspects of health. It may throw light on the way he was treated or taught as a child. His behaviour and manner may be the result of his background and upbringing. It can show how he approaches life, the career he chooses or where he directs his energies. Planets are found in this house are likely to have a strong influence.

The Second House

*Similar to Taurus and Venus, and
it is a Succedent house.*

This is concerned with personal possessions and personal finances, along with basic needs such as food, clothing and shelter. It is concerned with values, priorities and self-esteem, some aspects of the feelings and of relationships, and the five senses. Along with the first house, it can refer to a person's image.

The Third House

*This is similar to Gemini and Mercury, and
it is a Cadent house.*

This house rules brothers and sisters, cousins and other relatives of one's own generation, along with neighbours and local matters. Traditionally, it concerns local travel and short journeys but this could now be extended into any kind of travel that is normal for the subject. It rules communications and information of all kinds, plus paperwork, negotiations, and basic education. This house shows the capacity to think and such things as a talent for figure work or dexterity, or the lack of these things.

The Fourth House

*Similar to Cancer and the Moon, and
it is an angular house.*

In all but the equal house system, this house starts at the IC. This rules the parents, especially the mother figure or the person who nurtured the subject. It concerns the childhood home and domestic circumstances throughout life, as well as land or property matters. Traditionally, it represents the beginning and the end of life.

The Fifth House

*Similar to Leo and the Sun,
this is a Succedent house.*

This house rules anything that the subject creates, which may relate to artistry, music and creativity. It also rules the creation of a family and especially children. It rules pleasures, holidays and hobbies which are fun or amusing; love affairs and any spontaneous affection, such as that for pets, small children and so on. It also rules time off from the struggle of daily life, love affairs and fun.

The Sixth House

*Similar to Virgo and Mercury (also possibly, Chiron),
this is a cadent house.*

Traditionally, this is the house of employers and employees, so it has much to do with work and duty. This house also rules health and prevention of illness, food and the harvest, and duties to others. It's associated with pets, especially small animals.

The Seventh House

*Similar to Libra and Venus,
this is an angular house.*

This house is linked to open relationships and all that happens in connection with them, so it rules marriage and partnerships but also open enemies. This house rules business partnerships and agreements, and many kinds of legal agreements between two parties, such as contracts and so on.

The Eighth House

*Similar to Scorpio, Pluto and Mars,
this is a Succedent house.*

This house is connected with those heavy-duty turning points in life, such as birth, death, marriage, divorce and commitments of all kinds. It links to shared resources and other people's money, which in turn concerns such things as banking, legacies, taxes, corporate matters and everything linked to the care of other people's goods or those that are shared. It can rule dealings with the police, crime and forensics, as well as surgery. Resentment and hatred are hidden in his house, as are sexual secrets and even hidden abuse of many kinds. This house can show karmic difficulties.

The Ninth House

*Similar to Sagittarius and Jupiter,
this is a cadent house.*

This house is concerned with escape, freedom and expanding one's horizons, so it denotes foreign travel and dealings with foreign people and goods. It can relate to business that crosses frontiers. It tests limits, which means that it's concerned with the law and the rules of religion and belief. It links to further education and an interest in spiritual and philosophic matters. This house is said to connect to a dealings with large animals, gambling and sports.

The Tenth House

*Similar to Capricorn and Saturn,
this is an Angular house.*

In all but the equal house system, this house starts at the MC. It rules the subject's aims and ambitions, what he or she would like to achieve in life and the status that the person strives to reach. It is linked to parents, especially father figures, and to people in authority who can be helpful or obstructive. It can rule the subject's immediate circle along with his or her achievements, responsibilities and public image (along with the first and second houses). This house represents limiting circumstances and limits to opportunity.

The Eleventh House

*Similar to Aquarius, Uranus and Saturn,
this is a Succedent house.*

This house rules friends and acquaintances, and detached or more distant relationships. It's also associated with education and the acquisition of knowledge. It concerns activities that affect groups of people, such as clubs, societies, unions, workshops, political groups and so on. It can be associated with intellectual pleasures such as crosswords, but also astrology. It shows the person's hopes and wishes.

The Twelfth House

*Similar to Pisces, Neptune and Jupiter,
this is a Cadent house.*

This house rules service to others, self-sacrifice and care for the weak. It also concerns self-undoing, escapism, the mystical side of life and the occult. It talks of the unconscious and therefore of deeply hidden urges or needs, also the need to escape through alcohol or drugs. It is associated sensitivity, creativity and artistry, sports and music.

Chapter Fifteen: Planets in Houses

The planets don't work in quite the same way in the houses as they do in the signs. The sign modifies the character of the planet, but the house shows how the planet is used. For example, Mercury in Virgo is analytical in character, but when in the second house, it would be used to gain wealth or to conserve one's money or possessions, and in the ninth house, it would be used to stretch the mind and gain a good education or to travel for study or business.

The Sun

First House

These subjects are concerned with themselves and the projection of their personalities. They can be sunny, cheerful and fun. They achieve some kind of celebrity. They enjoy the company of children and young people.

Second House

Centred on money and possessions, these subjects should be wealthy. They are materialistic or they may simply want a comfortable life. They have a high earning capacity and can be possessive over goods or people. They are cautious over decisions and they usually seek harmonious relationships with others.

Third House

Fluent talkers who need to communicate. They may work in journalism, the media, teaching or writing, or they may deal with neighbourhood matters. These people can be closely attached to sisters, brothers and cousins. They can lack patience and consistency.

Fourth House

These subjects are interested in home and family and they will help family members. They are conscious of background and family history and may take up genealogy or history as a hobby. They may be collectors. Many choose to work from home. They have a caring personality but they can be shy or withdrawn. Some of them lose out on parental love in childhood. Excellent listeners.

Fifth House

These subjects can be over-generous. They need to enjoy life to the full but may want more than is possible. They are very fond of children. They may be musical, creative or sporty. Some have many love affairs while others are unusually faithful· to one partner. Stubborn. They are drawn to showbiz and glamorous professions.

Sixth House

Hardworking with good organising ability and a head for details but forgetful about things that don't interest them.

These people are health conscious and they can be hypochondriacs. They can be difficult and exacting, and they are better talkers than listeners.

Seventh House

These subjects want to be liked. They enjoy marriage and working partnerships. They want to express themselves but they may do what others dictate. These subjects may be lazy or prefer to lean on others who make decisions for them. Good looking, musical, creative, popular.

Eighth House

Interested in the afterlife, possibly involved in deeds, wills and official matters related to life and death. These subjects can be interested in medicine, forensic investigation, detective work or the occult. These people have powerful but difficult personalities. They may be involved with other people's finances.

Ninth House

Many of these subjects choose to live in different countries from those in which they grew up. They are tolerant of different cultures and they may have a flair for languages. Broadminded outlook. They may be attracted to religion, education or the law. Some choose to work with animals, while others become involved in publishing or broadcasting.

Tenth House

Interested in career, status, advancement, politics and public image. They may have a vocation that causes them to neglect family and friends, because they are hardworking, dedicated and somewhat austere.

Eleventh House

May officiate in clubs and societies or work for the betterment of humanity. Friendly and open-minded, they try to make others happy. They can be detached in personal relationships and not particularly fond of family life.

Twelfth House

These subjects may work alone and they may also choose to live alone. They are very sensitive and introverted. These people need their own home comforts and if they must have people around them, they choose people they know well and whom they can trust. They may be interested in art, music and creative pursuits and they may want to escape from reality from time to time. These people are interested in the occult and they may be quite clairvoyant. They may have hidden sides to their personality that only comes out after living or working with them for a while.

The Moon

First House

These subjects are strongly affected by their mothers and the relationship is either very good or pretty awful, but always unforgettable. The emotions are strong and the subject is sensitive, but the feelings and emotions can be suppressed, especially in males. These people can take their anguish out on a partner, or try to heal the world or put the environment to rights. Childhood experiences can lead to difficult behaviour patterns in adult life. This may be eased if the Moon is in a feminine sign or if it is well aspected. It can indicate a talent for art or music, an interest in the food trades, or a desire to save the planet. The sign which is rising is strongly emphasised and the effects of the Moon will be coloured by whatever sign is involved.

Second House

These subjects need security, so they may save or collect articles of value. They may simply surround themselves with clutter in order to feel safe and secure. These people have good business instincts but their income and their luck can ebb and flow. Their feelings towards their loved ones are very strong and they can be possessive.

Third House

Attached to their siblings or to a neighbourhood that they know well. They may take responsibility for other family members. Their early education is unsettled and they may never really find it easy to concentrate deeply or to stick to one idea.

Fourth House

Maternal and home loving, these subjects may demand more love and affection than anyone can reasonably give them. They may cling to old lovers, children, friends and their past. They are loyal to their family and friends. These people may be interested in history or objects with a provenance. Some choose to work from home, or to work with children in a family atmosphere.

Fifth House

Outgoing and rather dramatic or over-emotional, they may be attracted to a glamorous lifestyle, possibly in the world of the arts, the stage or sports. Alternatively, they might fill their homes and their lives with children. They may marry someone who has children or they may teach.

Sixth House

These subjects may have been ailing in childhood, or they may be obsessed by health, hygiene or food. They may work from home or move to be close to their work. They may grow up with a demanding mother or they may in their turn be difficult to live with. The may have to cope with a chronic illness.

Seventh House

May be vulnerable and dependent, needing a maternal partner or they may try to smother or control others. They are very interested in business matters and they make successful working partnerships.

Eighth House

Interested in psychic or intuitive subjects with strong powers of ESP. They may be preoccupied with life, death and the spiritual side of things. Sex is another strong interest for these subjects. These people may become involved in public finances or they may be strongly influenced by a partner's financial position. They have a talent for business and can be extremely successful in business partnerships.

Ninth House

They have many interests, particularly ecology, animals, legal matters and spirituality. May pursue an interest in a variety of esoteric interests and they may be keen on languages. They usually travel a good deal and they may choose to live or work in a different country from the one in which they grew up. Some marry foreigners. They may write or broadcast.

Tenth House

These subjects work very hard, either because they want to or because they have to in order to keep their families and homes in tact. Life can be hard. Their careers may take precedence over their private lives. They may be drawn to politics or public service and they may achieve wealth or fame, although this can be at the cost of their family life. Their families may be drawn into their public worlds (such as a politician's husband or wife).

Eleventh House

These subjects are keen on friends, clubs and group activities, so they are very sociable but not always so keen on family life. Some are happier at work than at home. Their objectives are changeable and their interests varied. They have many friends and acquaintances.

Twelfth House

These subjects need time (sometimes years) in order to cope with their childhoods and their feelings towards parents, previous spouses or other members of their families. They may learn hard lessons through relatives. They appear tough but they are very soft inside and they are easily hurt. In some cases, the proximity of the Moon to the ascendant makes these subjects similar to those who have the Moon in the first house. There may be a hidden and unresolved problem that has been left over from the subject's childhood.

Mercury

First House

These subjects are clever and literate but if Mercury is afflicted, they can find thinking, talking or writing difficult. Similarly, they can be computer and accounts wizards or unable to cope with numbers. They try to make an intellectual impact on the world. They can speak without thinking and hurt others with their words. They can push their friends and relatives away by this behaviour. Some overrule feelings with logic, while others are too self-centred.

Second House

Businesslike and business-minded. Possibly large scale wheeler-dealers. Practical and dexterous. Good craftsmen or musicians. Interested in food and cookery.

Third House

Keen on education, good teachers. They may be closely involved with brothers and sisters, neighbours or neighbourhood matters. Local travel and vehicles could figure strongly in their lives. They may release pent up tension by writing poetry or music.

Fourth House

These subjects are fond of their home surroundings and they may choose to work from home. Maternal and domesticated, they make a point of talking and listening to their children and they are also keen on educating them.

These people may be interested in history or collecting things that have a past. They can work from home.

Fifth House

May teach or be intellectually involved with children. Good at intellectual games but easily bored by work that requires attention to detail or a rigid routine. They want both love and sex, and they see sex as an essential part of communication but they also need conversation.

Sixth House

These subjects have very analytical minds and they make excellent secretaries. They can be academic, musical or good at craft and design. They may be nervous, fussy or health-conscious. They find it hard to plan or to look forward with optimism, and they may suffer from a low sense of self-esteem. Some talk incessantly about nothing.

Seventh House

These subjects seek an intellectual rapport with others. They are good friends and also excellent diplomats or liaison officers. They have a good attitude to marriage and working partnerships. They may be better talkers than listeners. Some are excellent designers or craftsmen. If Mercury is afflicted, these subjects may be prone to illness.

Eighth House

Successful businessmen and women who have clever ideas. They are deep thinkers. They may be interested in the occult, religion and the afterlife. They may be keen on reading or writing thrillers or working in the undertaking industry. Their emotions are deep but they may be expressed in an intellectual manner. They have good concentration but afflicted Mercury can cause blockages in the thinking processes.

Ninth House

Good students and teachers with a flair for English or foreign languages. They may have too many ideas to bring any of them to fruition and they need to apply themselves conscientiously.

Tenth House

Can be drawn to a career in communications or a business that has a communicative basis. They need a mental outlet or they can become unhappy or frustrated.

Eleventh House

These subjects enjoy being involved with clubs and societies and they have many friends. They are approachable and friendly, although they can be sarcastic and tactless at times. They have wide-ranging ideas about politics.

Twelfth House

Inward looking and secretive, their inner feelings are very important to them. They are sensitive, thoughtful and kind. Some are attracted to mysticism and they may write or compose music on these themes. These people may have problems in connection with their work or their health and they need a happy and stable marriage in order to function successfully.

Venus

First House

Good looking. This is a good placement for models, starlets or work in the fashion or glamour industry. Interested in art, music, fashion, hair and makeup, and things of beauty. They enjoy flattery. They can become wealthy. Has charm.

Second House

Could collect or create attractive and valuable artefacts. Could be interested in the arts or the business side of art or beauty. Clever business people who are materialistic. May be interested in craftwork, fashion, makeup, cookery and gardening. Sensual and charming.

Third House

Sociable and friendly. They get on well with siblings, relatives and neighbours. Could attract wealthy or influential friends or colleagues. Can study successfully, especially if the chosen subject has an artistic, musical, cultural or beauty bias. Could be extravagant, especially where the family is concerned. Could collect valuable items of an intellectual nature, such as books. They make good agents or liaison officers.

Fourth House

These subjects make beautiful homes with lovely decor, flower arrangements, etc. Could be extravagant, especially where the family is concerned. Could be successful antique collectors or dealers. Could succeed in the fields of insurance, property or small businesses. Could have wealthy parents, especially the mother.

Fifth House

Children are liked, may work with them in some way. These subjects' children should become rich or successful in some glamorous industry. Love of glamour and the fun side of life. Could enjoy flirtation, love affairs, travel, games, sports, gambling and all kinds of amusements and treats. May be very creative and artistic, also fond of music. Could have very creative children.

Sixth House

These subjects need to work in pleasant surroundings with good working conditions. May choose a glamorous career. They dislike hard physical or dirty work. May be health-conscious, but basically strong, unless Venus is afflicted. Will gain money and influence through work.

Seventh House

These people could marry for money but even if they marry for love, they could still find themselves in easy circumstances as a result. Good placement for a happy marriage or for marriage to a successful partner. Affectionate and loving, but needing validation and encouragement from others.

Eighth House

Very intense and rather jealous feelings. May inherit or marry money. Could make career out of the police, medical, or some other kind of diagnostic or investigative work.

Ninth House

These subjects will well at school or university and they will certainly enjoy their time there. They may partner people from other countries. May make money from the travel trade or will travel for fun. May inherit money or obtain it through a second marriage or through in-laws. Could become happily involved in spiritual or religious matters, possibly through marriage. May make a career in the law, arbitration or liaison work.

Tenth House

These subjects should have happy and successful careers, especially in something that makes money and also brings fame. Could work in a feminine or glamour career. Good manner with people, especially in business. Could make money by being associated with influential people.

Eleventh House

Diplomatic, discreet and good with people. Could be happy working for clubs, societies or with specialised groups of people. Clever politicians. Could have rich or influential friends.

Twelfth House

Attracted to the occult or to mysticism. May have secret love affairs or a need for seclusion and time alone. Creative, imaginative, artistic and musical.

Mars

First House

These subjects have assertive personalities and they may be pushy, domineering and difficult. Alternatively, the Mars energy can be channelled into sport, adventure, the military life, pioneering or exploration. They may be impulsive, passionate, reckless and full of daring. These subjects can have red hair and a hot temper to go with it. Alternatively, they may have a mole, wart, strawberry or other mark on the head or face. They can suffer from headaches, head injuries or high blood pressure.

Second House

Aggressive money-makers who are competitive in business or in any sphere where land, possessions and money are concerned. They may have wonderful singing voices or simply loud voices that they use to dominate a conversation. These subjects can be high earners but they can also be extravagant. The throat is sensitive.

Third House

These subjects could be keen students both at school and later in life. They have quick and active minds. These people are protective towards their families and, either especially close to, or antagonistic towards their siblings. They can be argumentative or verbally aggressive. Alternatively, they may use words purpose fully as part of a job, for instance as a writer, broadcaster or salesperson. These subjects are unlikely to be attracted to a slow or stupid partner. The arms, shoulders, wrists and hands are weak points, as are the lungs.

Fourth House

These subjects work hard in the home and are very attached to their homes and families. This placement can be a considerably softening factor in a hard and aggressive chart but it can be the worst thing in the world in a soft chart. These subjects may enjoy carpentry, car maintenance and so on. They may move house fairly frequently and they may make money out of property. They can be quarrelsome in the home or they may simply shout rather ineffectually at their spouses and children. They may whine about supposed problems or about their health. They need to connect with the loved one on the deepest level. The breasts, lungs and stomachs are sensitive.

Fifth House

These subjects are usually strong and robust. They are keen on sports and games and may be very competitive. They make excellent salesmen and women. They can be pushy parents who want their children to compete and to win. They are good with children and young people and they may work or spend their spare time with them. Passion may be channelled into work or creativity rather than lovemaking. The back and heart are weak spots.

Sixth House

These subjects can work very hard when their interest is aroused but they can switch off and simply serve time if their jobs don't hold their interest. Some are hard on subordinates, using their considerable communications skills to cutting effect, while others with this placement are very kind and thoughtful to other people. These people make good critics and they can use their critical skills to hurt or to amuse. Some of them talk incessantly, others are 'nit-pickers' but, to be hottest, they bring more pain to themselves than they do to others. The skin, bowels and intestines may be sensitive.

Seventh House

An energetic attitude to marriage and partnerships. Can be quarrelsome and the cause of their own disappointments in relationships. Some people with this placement wait for others to validate them because they have no clear idea of their own worth. Passionate. The kidneys, bladder and other internal organs can be weak.

Eighth House

Attracted to the medical profession, especially surgery. Butchery is another possible career as are mining, engineering, the armed forces or weaponry. Can be keen on detection and investigation, forensic or insurance matters. There may be a deep interest in death or the afterlife. These subjects can be passionate, jealous and possibly conscience-ridden. They may have health problems relating to the reproductive organs or the lower back. The throat can be sensitive too.

Ninth House

These subjects are more active than intellectual. They make good sportspeople or adventurers, being interested in travel, often to unknown regions. They love to hunt, and may chase the opposite sex. These people have a well-developed sense of fair play and they may be keen lawyers. They may choose to work in the travel trade or the legal, educational, literary or religious professions. Their hips and legs may be weak spots.

Tenth House

Can be hard, energetic workers who reach the top alone. These subjects can be ruthlessly ambitious. They may be attracted to politics, engineering or the armed forces. Very big business enterprises attract them, as does banking. Depending upon other factors on the chart, these people have good family relationships. Others can concentrate their energies on their ambitions. Their weak spots are the skin, ears, teeth, bones, knees and shins.

Eleventh House

Clubs and societies are liked and group work or group activities of all kinds appeal. These subjects make wonderfully enthusiastic friends but they can fall out with others just as quickly as they fall in with them. They are attracted to causes and may be interested in politics. The ankles and circulation are the weak spots.

Twelfth House

These subjects live a rich inner life and they will spend some part of their lives on an inward or spiritual journey. They don't have an aggressive bone in their bodies and they may be unassertive and self-sacrificial. Their weak spots are their feet and legs, their circulation and, in some cases, their lungs or body fluids.

Jupiter

First House

Broad-minded and cheerful. These subjects are lucky in life, either making money easily or attaching themselves to partners who become rich. Attracted to travel, education, publishing and broadcasting, religion or the law. They learn a great deal about whatever is represented by the sign that this planet occupies.

Second House

These subjects are lucky with money and possessions, but while they can make money easily but they may be too generous or open-handed to keep it. They can earn money dealing with foreigners or foreign goods. Landowning, farming, animal husbandry or some other form of outdoor life can feature in their lives.

Third House

These subjects get on well with their brothers and sisters. They are quite studious successful academically at school or later in life. They have a deep interest in communications and they may write or travel as part of their working lives.

Fourth House

Good relationships with parents and a good home life characterise this placement. May move house often or may make money out of property matters. Some inherit property while others win a share in property through the courts. They can lack perspective or be too closely focused on home or family matters. Some work from their homes in some way.

Fifth House

All forms of speculation are lucky for these subjects and they are good at sports and the creative arts. They may make money from sports, art or some kind of glamour business. They may enjoy working with children. They are religious or spiritual and they may teach in a Sunday school. These subjects may have a dramatic, larger-than-life manner and they may be reckless and easily bored. Their children do well and can have lucky lives in their turn.

Sixth House

These subjects are happy at work and they enjoy what they do. They make money from working and they could inherit a business. They may work in travel, the law, education and religion. Travel interests them and they are fond of animals. Hips and thighs may be weak or may suffer from accidents if other factors on the chart point to this.

Seventh House

This is an excellent placement for partnerships both of the working and the personal kind. Marriage may be either very good or very bad. These subjects are friendly and flirtatious and they are especially attracted to foreigners or anyone who is different in some way. Pleasant and patient personalities.

Eighth House

There is a strong chance that these subjects could inherit money. There may be a particularly easy or casual attitude towards death and the afterlife. These subjects may do very well from marriage and they could be attracted to partners from other countries or who are unusual.

Ninth House

These subjects may travel a lot or be interested in religious or spiritual matters. They may teach or work in the law, publishing or the media. These people are happy, lucky and sometimes reckless. They can be outspoken, eccentric or tactless. Their hips and thighs may be weak.

Tenth House

These subjects do well in their chosen career and may achieve public acclaim. They can be successful without making a great deal of effort. These people may have a rather dramatic personality. They may need a good deal of variety in their working lives. They want to leave the world a better or a happier place than when they found it.

Eleventh House

These subjects have many friends and acquaintances, some of them being rich and influential. They may have a strangely casual or a pompously high-minded attitude to others. They may embrace causes and they may use their wealth philanthropically.

Twelfth House

These people prefer to work alone and they may achieve success in something like poetry, art or dancing. They like the sea and are keen on travel. These subjects are also interested in medicine. They are talented and musical, but shy.

Saturn

First House

These subjects' parents may have had difficulty in conceiving them or giving birth. They may be conscious of having lived before and of not wanting to come back again. These people are serious, hard working and ambitious. They take life seriously and they take a responsible attitude to all that they do. This placement can lead to fame and fortune!

Second House

These subjects work hard to make money and they succeed in due course. Success is hard-won but almost inevitable. They can be possessive and stingy.

Third House

A hard early life with problems at school, but success and self-education come later through their own efforts. They help their brothers and sisters and have good relations with neighbours.

Fourth House

An unhappy and deprived early life. Could have restrictive parents who may have been stingy or cruel. These subjects work hard to obtain a good family and home of their own and they value these things when they have them. Their early problems may not have been due to bad parenting but to poverty or tribulation in the family.

Fifth House

These subjects may have a domineering parent (usually the father). They may lack joy, or they may work too hard and forget how to play. Alternatively, they may take a serious attitude to creative endeavours and make a great success out of these. Children may be seen as a burden but they are loved and can become successful in their turn. Some people with this placement choose not to have children or they may have difficulty in producing children.

Sixth House

There may be difficulty in connection with childbirth or with a sick child. I have found that Saturn placed here can bring difficulties in either having children or bringing them up. These subjects may suffer with bad backs or arthritis.

Seventh House

These people may marry late or marry someone who is much older or much younger than them. There may be restriction or frustration in marriage or as a result of marriage or business partnerships. They are faithful partners with a serious attitude to the partnership or frankly not interested in the partner.

Eighth House

A careful, responsible attitude to money, especially when dealing with other people's resources, but can be morbid and miserable. On the other hand, all these areas of life may work out well once the subject gets into middle age.

Ninth House

Deep thinkers who are dedicated to causes that benefit mankind. These subjects are happier when they get older. Long-distance travel and foreigners may bring them trouble but also status or money. These subjects may spend a lifetime searching for spiritual experiences or some kind of meaning to their lives.

Tenth House

Could be ambitious to the exclusion of social and family life. Obligations can weigh heavily. These subjects may be efficient and conscientious at work despite not enjoying their work. They may switch career in mid-life and achieve a great deal of success later on. They may achieve fame and fortune or suffer public disgrace.

Eleventh House

These subjects may take committees and group activities very seriously. They may have influential friends. Alternatively, they may be too busy with their jobs to have any friends. Elderly relatives and friends may help them to get on in life.

Twelfth House

This placement can lead to sadness and also to mental problems or an inability to express thoughts. These people may find themselves married to a partner who doesn't talk or listen to them. They may feel lonely even when surrounded by family. They may be their own worst enemy. Some turn early suffering, an ailing childhood or their own super-sensitivity to suffering to advantage by becoming nurses, counsellors, astrologers or carers. These subjects learn to discipline their inner selves and may learn to cope by using meditative techniques.

Uranus

First House

Intelligent, unpredictable, individualistic. Should have a modern, scientific mind but may have unusual ideas or an unusual lifestyle. May have nerve or circulation problems. Friends could be extremely important to these subjects.

Second House

Unpredictable income. These subjects may have gains and losses on a grand scale or they may have two or more different sources of income. Sudden loss or gains of job or an unusual way of gaining possessions, resources. Non-materialist attitude to life. Friends may help these subjects find something that they value in life, but their values would be unusual in any case.

Third House

Frequent changes of school or an unusual education. Lively, intelligent mind with unusual ideas. Odd experiences regarding brothers and sisters. May become close to friends and treat them like brothers and sisters. Friends may educate these subjects.

Fourth House

Unstable situation early in life, with many upheavals or changes of home. May have behaved badly as a child. May choose to live in an unusual home, or under strange circumstances later in life. May choose to make a home with a friend.

Fifth House

May have love affairs or affairs with friends who become lovers and then slip back to being friends once again. Friends offer inspiration. Lively, intelligent mind, possibly an inventor; certainly creative in an unusual way. Could have unusual pastimes or hobbies. Will have clever children.

Sixth House

Can be unpredictable at work. May have two jobs, or one very unusual one. May have sudden illnesses, such as circulation problems or paralysis. May have many friends at or through work.

Seventh House

An unusual and very free marriage is needed. Must have mental rapport with the partner. Could choose unusual partners. Working partnerships could be very odd. Could choose to live with a friend and have sexual relationships away from the home.

Eighth House

Unusual, ideas in the realm of work, money and sex. Could gain and lose money from business partnerships or marriage circumstances. May inherit. May be attached to a strange partner. May have an unusual attitude to friends.

Ninth House

Could spend a lot of time travelling and have great gains and losses as a result. Could be a very lucky gambler.

Accident-prone and also prone to mental stress. Could be an excellent clairvoyant or medium. May be keen on helping groups of people to understand religion and spirituality. Could make friends through hobbies, interests or while travelling.

Tenth House

Possible sudden changes in career, because these subjects dislike routine. Far-sighted with leadership qualities. May have two jobs that are equally important to each other, but very different from one another. May make good friends at work or choose to work with groups of friends. May work with or for groups of people. Keen on education in order to get on in life. May work as astrologers.

Eleventh House

Fond of clubs, societies and group activities. They have many friends but they gain and lose them quickly. These people might be eccentric or different in some way. May be keen astrologers. Far-sighted, broad-minded, these people never stop educating themselves.

Twelfth House

These subjects may have terrific clairvoyant abilities and they may be keen on astrology. Secretive, they may harbour odd ideas and feelings. Could be very spiritual and mystical or eccentric. These people may hide their emotions or they may be confused by them or be upset by feelings of inner turmoil.

Neptune

First House

These subjects are dreamy, sensitive and artistic. They may be impractical, disorganised, chaotic and forgetful. Some are eccentric, whereas others are drawn to mystical or artistic pursuits. They are often talented, musical or artistic and some make excellent photographers. May like the sea and fishing.

Second House

May not be able to keep money for long, or possibly mean and money-minded. Usually non-materialistic in outlook. These subjects value kindness and caring for others. They may make money from mystical or other unusual interests. They may work successfully in something to do with liquids such as the oil industry, sailing, fishing, shipping, plumbing, etc. They like aesthetic or artistic objects.

Third House

These subjects are intuitive and imaginative. They may lack concentration or they may have a wonderful gift of communication through visual effects (video, photography) or through descriptive writing. Could work as a therapist. Good actor, but may be something of a drifter.

Fourth House

These subjects may love their homes but they may not keep them very tidy. Alternatively, the home may be a thing of great beauty. There should be a good relationship with the parents with an intuitive, telepathic link. May be disorganised in practical matters, but with a strong imagination or inner life.

Fifth House

Very creative and imaginative. Could have a career on the stage or something similar. These subjects tend to be escapist at times, they may prefer television and books to real life or they may simply have a strong inner life. Fond of dancing and of the sea. May love wild countryside, and trees in particular. Should have excellent rapport with small children and a good relationship with their own children.

Sixth House

Can be very creative and may work hard on their chosen projects, but otherwise, they can be lazy and uninterested in work. Interested in humanitarian causes or working in an artistic or mystical sphere. May work as a nurse, with the mentally-handicapped, or a similar kind of occupation. May have allergies. May be drawn to work near water or with liquids (cooking, hairdressing).

Seventh House

These subjects either have wonderfully happy marriages or confused and difficult ones. They may be very independent or they may lean heavily on their partners. They may have vague attitudes to life or they may be quite sensible but with a tendency to draw drunken or chaotic people to them. They may have an idealised vision of relationships. They would be taken for a ride in any kind of business or working partnership.

Eighth House

Could be very psychic and drawn to the world of mysticism, the occult or to spiritualism. Very intuitive and mediumistic, more in touch with the other side than here for much of the time. Could squander inheritance or a partner's money or alternatively a partner may take them for a fool. They may choose an artistic partner and/or enjoy an absolutely ideal relationship where sex is elevated to a spiritual fuel. They may have strange love affairs with peculiar people.

Ninth House

Could work in the fields of philosophy or religion. May be inspired. May do well in trades connected to the sea or to liquids, such as the oil industry, hairdressing, etc. Could travel a great deal and could fall in love while travelling. May be involved in strange legal cases that go on for years. These subjects help people who are in trouble or who cannot help themselves.

Tenth House

These subjects may choose a career for idealistic reasons. They may work in feminine or creative fields such as photography, art, dancing, poetry or something similar. Alternatively, they could choose nursing, working with prisoners, the mentally-handicapped, or in some other form of caring occupation. They aspire to something greater than simply earning money and they want to heal the world. Some work with liquids such as oil, the sea or the alcohol industry. They may go through many changes in life and they could be greatly helped or let down by others in career matters. May start off well and then let everything come to naught.

Eleventh House

Idealistic, artistic and creative, these subjects may find it hard to get anything done at all. Their aims are intellectual and artistic and they are keen on groups who have the same kind of goal. Could be greatly helped or badly let down by friends. May be mystical, intuitive and interested in astrology.

Twelfth House

Likely to be interested in poetry, ballet, culture, art and music. Could be a great animal lover or a lover of people, especially those who need help. Mystical, spiritual and other-worldly. May have great sadness in life or simply be drawn inwards to a contemplative existence.

Pluto

First House

These subjects have attractive, magnetic personalities and dynamic natures. They are attracted to big business or to positions of power and authority. Their lives go in distinct phases with gains and losses every few years. Can brood and have a terrible temper. They tend to control or rule others if they can. They lose people through death, their families or they may have brushes with death. Resentful and possibly jealous or suffer from the jealousy of others.

Second House

Can make very big money, but may lose it on a grand scale, too. These subjects have a good grasp of business affairs. They also have a deep need for security, and may see money and possessions as a form of this. They can be covetous or they may be hoarders.

Third House

These subjects have terrific powers of concentration and they finish the projects that they start. They can be moody and depressed at times. They may do much to help their siblings or, alternatively, they can be beastly to them. These people can make money by teaching and writing and they enjoy influencing others via the medium of words.

Fourth House

These people feel very deeply about their homes, their parents and their marriage partners. They may try to control or dominate their families and they may be too fond of their own point of view when· in the home situation. They may inherit property.

Fifth House

Children are important to these subjects and they may go to a lot of trouble, either to have children or to bring them up. They may live for pleasure or they may take a serious view of pastimes, sports and so on. These people enjoy the arts and music, and they could be drawn to gambling in order to make money. Some have many affairs while others put their energies into creative schemes.

Sixth House

May be a very hard worker or may simply be too concerned with working life. These people try to reform or change their colleagues' working practices. They may have weak health or irritable bowels and some of these problems may be due to tension.

Seventh House

Could be very good business partners but a bit overbearing. Could be demanding marriage partners, with too much emphasis on sex. Feelings are intense and jealousy is a problem, but these subjects may be on the receiving end of this kind of treatment rather than dishing it out themselves. May inherit from a partner.

Eighth House

Very intuitive, especially where money and business is concerned. May inherit from a partner. May work for the community or in a mediumistic or spiritual manner. Could be very keen on Plutonic interests such as the afterlife, death, sex, birth, medical or forensic and investigative matters. Could deal with the insides or the underneath of things, e.g. butchery, mining or simply digging out secrets. Very secretive themselves. Analytical, logical, with very searching minds. Could be animal lovers. Resentful.

Ninth House

Very spiritual. These people may be bound up with foreigners or distant places. They may force their religious or spiritual views on others, or they may drag others through the courts. Could be very keen on educating themselves and others. Could be very fond of animals, or keen to travel to strange places.

Tenth House

These subjects can reach great heights of influence or they can attach themselves to influential people. They may work in fields where they can influence others or even take them over in some way. For instance, this is a good placement for hypnotherapists, anaesthetists and dream analysts. There may be powerful urges to rule and these subjects may be obsessed with dreams of grandeur. May be attracted to drugs or may work with them. Dynamic, powerful or nuts.

Eleventh House

These people may be looking for the truth and may choose astrology as a method for doing this. These subjects may have powerful and influential friends or they may try to influence groups of people or to make friends of people in order to change or influence them. Mainly well-balanced and sensible, although with one or two funny ideas from time to time.

Twelfth House

These subjects have hidden talents and interests. They may go in for hidden or taboo love affairs of some sort. They may have hidden problems of a psychological kind, such as suppressed anger or hatred for something that has been done to them by others. They may strive to find some kind of mystical or astrological truth and to express this to others in the form of poetry or music.

Chiron

First House

Could have health problems in the head, brain, eyes or upper jaw. May have a difficult personality that alienates others, or may have to put up with someone like this in life.

Second House

Health problems related to the lower jaw, throat and neck. May find it difficult to obtain or keep money and goods. May be over-generous.

Third House

May have health problems in connection with the bronchial tubes, shoulders, arms or hands, while the nervous system may be vulnerable. May find school difficult or have difficult brothers or sisters.

Fourth House

May have weak lungs or chest area, or digestive problems. The home life may be difficult. May have an unpleasant mother or mother figures to contend with.

Fifth House

Health problems will concern the spine and heart. May have problems related to children or one or more children may be ill or disabled in some way.

Sixth House

May suffer with bowel problems or abdominal pain. Diabetes possible. The working life will be blocked and difficult at time.

Seventh House

May suffer with inner organs, such as the pancreas, kidneys and bladder. Diabetes possible. Troubled partnerships both of a personal and a work kind.

Eighth House

May suffer with the reproductive organs or lower abdomen and lower spine. Relationships may be extremely difficult at times and that goes for business or financial ones as well as romantic ones. Sex may cause some kind of problem.

Ninth House

May suffer with hip and thigh problems, also liver trouble. May feel trapped and need to escape a bad situation. Grandparents may be difficult or second marriage could be difficult. Lack of higher education or qualifications. May have to deal with religious people who cause pain and difficulty.

Tenth House

Bones, hearing, teeth and skin will cause difficulties, along with possible asthma and eczema. The knees and shins may also be vulnerable. Blockages to career and in achieving aims and ambitions.

Eleventh House

There may be a problem with the ankles, skin, breathing, hearing, teeth and bones. Friends may need help or they may be fine until they turn on the subject and cause him a deep hurt.

Twelfth House

The feet, lungs, brain, nerves and mind may cause problems. Could be assailed by psychic events of some strange kind. Very imaginative, and drawn to healing and helping others. May suffer times of isolation or intense loneliness.

~~~~~~~~~~

Ceres and Vesta

Both of these asteroids can bring peace in the home, or bounty of some kind, to the area of the chart that they touch.

Nodes of the Moon

There are many views on these, but the majority of astrologers consider the north node to be a point where life is difficult and lessons need to be learned, while the south is an easy area.

Chapter Sixteen: Aspects

Hard and Soft Aspects

Hard aspects aren't automatically bad or difficult, because this simply means that a planet is in conjunction, square or opposition to another planet or to the ascendant, descendant, midheaven or the nadir. These are the aspects that we are most likely to become aware of during the course of our lives.

Soft aspects, such as the sextile and trine are pleasant but others such as the inconjunct and semi-square can be awkward, so once again the terms refer to the geometrical type of aspect rather than the way it affects a subject.

Good and Bad Aspects

The words good, beneficial or easy can be applied to aspects that work well for the subject, while difficult or challenging ones are building blocks that enable us to succeed, or they can be a handicap. Often it is by overcoming our limitations that we actually manage to succeed; therefore a bad aspect can turn out to be a blessing in disguise.

Allowable Orbs

It's rare that two planets make an exact aspect, so a few degrees either way are allowable. Astrologers used to disagree somewhat on the orbs but astrological software sets these by default so we no longer worry much about this. You can change the default settings on your computer if you feel strongly about this.

ASPECT	DISTANCE BETWEEN PLANETS	EFFECT
Conjunction	0 deg.	Mainly good. But depends upon the planets involved
Semi-sextile	30 deg.	Mild effect, usually good
Sextile	60 deg.	Good, especially for intellectual matters
Quintile	70 deg.	Supposed to endow the native with brains
Square	90 deg.	Very difficult
Trine	120 deg.	Good, especially for family or creative matters
Inconjunct	150 deg.	Awkward and irritating
Opposition	180 deg.	Usually difficult, but there may be help from other people

The Aspects

Also Worth Mentioning

A 'Yod' aspect takes its name from a Hebrew letter that is a kind of 'Y' shape, and it means a double inconjunct, which happens when one planet is 150 degrees away from a planet in one direction and 150 degrees away from another planet in the other direction. This can be extremely irritating, and it may have an effect on the health of the person, or the financial aspects of his relationships with others.

There are several minor aspects, such as the bi-quintile, sesquiquadrate and others, but I suggest you leave these for now. Minor aspects and any aspect to the nodes of the moon should have a tight orb of no more than a couple of degrees.

Chapter Seventeen: The Body and Astrology

Signs, Planets and the Body

- Aries and Mars rule the head, eyes and brain.
- Taurus and Venus rule the throat and neck, along with the lower jaw.
- Gemini and Mercury rule the bronchial tubes, shoulders, arms and hands.
- Cancer and the Moon rule the lungs, digestion and breasts.
- Leo and the Sun rule the spine and heart.
- Virgo and Mercury (or possibly Chiron) rule the bowels.
- Libra and Venus rule the bladder and kidneys, along with mobility matters.
- Scorpio and Pluto rule the base of the spine and the reproductive organs.
- Sagittarius and Jupiter rule the hips, thighs and liver.
- Capricorn and Saturn rule the skin, breathing, bones, hearing, knees and shins.
- Aquarius and Uranus rule the ankles and breathing.
- Pisces rules the feet, also the lungs and nerves.

Conclusion

I wrote the original version of this book under the title of 'The Planets' in the early 1990s, as part of a series of books that included 'Moon Signs', 'Rising Signs' and 'Sun Signs'. A few years later, the original publisher changed hands and the new owners showed little interest in producing or selling books on astrology and related subjects. Once their stock of books had sold out, they allowed the series to die off, but eventually, I was able to take back the rights to all my books. Since then, I've reworked and republished the best of those books, adding some of them to the new "Sasha Fenton's" series of astrology titles, of which this is the latest.

All my astrology books in this series are aimed at those who are interested in astrology and who want something that is easy to read and to understand. In these revised versions, I've taken pains to make the information even clearer and easier to grasp. So, wherever you are on your astrological journey, I hope you keep this book on your shelf and reach for it when you need to check on something about the planets in astrology. These days, there are thousands of books on astrology and it's hard to know what to read, but this book should give you practical help.

Good luck and best wishes,
Sasha Fenton

Index

A
Ancient Divisions 13
Angles, The 50
Asc 50
Ascendant 50
Ascendant, The 106
aspects, Hard 162
aspects, Minor 164
aspects, Soft 162
Aspects, The 164
Asteroids 105
Astro-Cartography 106
Astrocalc 5
Astrolabe World Ephemeris 4

B
bi-quintile 164
Big Brother 38

C
Ceres 8, 48, 161
Charon 11
Chiron 5, 11, 46
Chiron in Aries 102
Chiron Transits 105

D
Dee, Jon 3
Deimos 10
Descendant 50
Descendant, The 107
Detriment 13
dragon's head 49
dragon's tail 49
Dsc 50

E
Ecliptic 7
Elements, The 109
ephemeredes 4
equinox, spring 7
Eris 9
Exaltation 13
Exaltation, Degrees of 14

F
Fall 13
first cry 4

G
Gaia 37
Gauquelin, Michel 15

H
Heliocentric Charts 16
Hemispheres 108
Henry the Seventh 9
Hercules 46
horoscope 4
Houses, Planets in 120
Houses, The 113

I
IC 51

Immum Coeli 51
inconjunct, double 164

J
Jason 46
Jupiter 31
Jupiter in Aries 86

K
karma 49
Kepler 5
Kethu 49

M
Manta 46
Mars 29
Mars in Aries 82
MC 50
Medium Coeli 50
Mercury 23
Mercury in Aries 74
Midheaven 50
Midheaven, The 107
Midpoints 16
Minimoons 10
Moon 9
Moon in Aries 64
Moon, The 20
Morpheus 40
Mutual Reception 15

N
Nadir 51
Nadir, The 107
natal chart 4
Neptune 40
Neptune in Aries 97
Nodes of the Moon 8, 48, 161

North Node of the Moon 48

O
Oberon 40
Orbs, Allowable 163

P
Part of Fortune 51
Perseus 46
Phobos 10
Planet, Leading 15
Planet, Rising 14
Planet, Ruling 14
Planets 10
planets, "terrestrial" 10
planets, impersonal 12
planets, personal 12
Planets, Retrograde 12
planets, transpersonal 12
Planets, Unaspected 15
Pluto 43
Pluto in Gemini 100
precession of the equinoxes 7
Prometheus 46

R
Rahu 49
Raphael's Ephemeris 5
reincarnation 49
Rulership 13

S
Saturn 34
Saturn in Aries 89
Sensitive Points 51
sesquiquadrate 164
sidereal 8
signs, cardinal 111

signs, fixed 111
signs, mutable 111
Solar Fire 5
Solar System 8
South Node of the Moon 49
stellium 15
Sun 9
Sun in Aries 52
Sun, The 17

T
The Qualities 111
Titania 40
Tudor era 9

U
Uranus 37
Uranus in Aries 94

V
Venus 26
Venus in Aries 78
Vertex, The 51
Vesta 8, 48, 161

W
Wars of the Roses 9
Winstar 5
www.astrotheme.com 5

Y
Yod 164

Z
Zodiac 7
zodiac, tropical 7

Zambezi Publishing Ltd

We hope you have enjoyed reading this book. The Zambezi range of books includes titles by top level, internationally acknowledged authors on fresh, thought-provoking viewpoints in your favourite subjects. A common thread with all our books is the easy accessibility of content; we have no sleep-inducing tomes, just down-to-earth, easily digestible, credible books.

~~~~~

Please visit our website (www.zampub.com) to browse our full range of Lifestyle and Mind, Body & Spirit titles, and to discover what might spark your interest next...

~~~~~

www.ingramcontent.com/pod-product-compliance
Lightning Source LLC
LaVergne TN
LVHW051559070426
835507LV00021B/2665